RESOURCE
TEACHERS

A Changing Role in the Three-Block Model
of Universal Design for Learning

Jennifer Katz

PORTAGE & MAIN PRESS

Portage & Main Press gratefully acknowledges the financial support of the Province of Manitoba through the Department of Sport, Culture & Heritage and the Manitoba Book Publishing Tax Credit, and the Government of Canada through the Canada Book Fund (CBF) for our publishing activities.

Printed and bound in Canada by Friesens
Cover and interior design by Relish New Brand Experience Inc.

Library and Archives Canada Cataloguing in Publication

Katz, Jennifer, author
        Resource teachers : a changing role in the three-block model
of universal design for learning / Jennifer Katz.

Includes bibliographical references.
Issued in print and electronic formats.
ISBN 978-1-55379-501-8 (pbk.).--ISBN 978-1-55379-502-5 (pdf)

        1. Inclusive education. 2. Teaching. I. Title.

LC1200.K35 2013   371.9'046   C2013-906171-1
                                                           C2013-906172-X

21 20 19 18   3 4 5 6 7

PORTAGE &
MAIN PRESS

1-800-667-9673
www.portageandmainpress.com
Winnipeg, Manitoba
Treaty 1 Territory and homeland of the Métis Nation

FSC
www.fsc.org
MIX
Paper from
responsible sources
FSC® C016245

For Mitchell, Ryan, Philip, David, Stewart, Aaron, Mineesha, Tumsaa, Daniel, Josh, Xerius; and Jamie, Michael, Colin, and all the members of The Expert Group; for Justin and Samantha, and all the students who have shaped my teaching, my heart, and my soul — and for Jorel, who continues to be my inspiration and demonstrate what an inclusive world should be, this work is for you.

Table of Contents

Acknowledgments

This book is the result of many years following the path of special education — from teaching in segregated classrooms, to being a resource teacher in an inclusive school, to teaching in inclusive classrooms as a regular classroom teacher. Along the way, many people have facilitated my learning in ways that led to the formation of my pedagogy and, hence, to this book — but a few stand out along my path.

My Aunt Sheila started me on my journey to serving children with disabilities. My memories of her and her inspiration stay with me every moment of every day. My thanks to Susan Quinn and Art Pfeffer who, after my aunt's passing, kept me going on this journey as an educational assistant. To Kathyrn D'Angelo, Catriona Misfeldt, and Gina Rae, many thanks for introducing me to the neurodevelopmental framework of Mel Levine, and for mentoring me in the role of consultant. And without Pat Mirenda and Marion Porath, my advisors at UBC, this framework would never have been formed into a holistic pedagogy.

I was mentored by the best. As a young resource teacher, I worked alongside a master resource teacher, Ida Ollenberger, who more than any other individual is responsible for this work. It was Ida who taught me how to assess, how to build a learning profile on a student, and how to transfer that knowledge into an Individual Education Plan. I grew as a person and as a teacher under her tutelage. My gratitude to her is boundless.

To all the Portage & Main Press staff — Annalee, Catherine, Kirsten — and my editor Jean, thanks for supporting my passion and perfectionism, and for persevering!

The past few years have been intense and challenging. I could not have accomplished all the publications — two books, twelve study units, twelve reading assessment packages, thirteen articles — and taught courses, implemented UDL in many divisions or delivered three hundred workshops across the country and internationally without an incredible network of support. Thank you to the faculty at the University of Manitoba — particularly Zana, Charlotte, Rick, Dawn, and Richard — who both formally and personally have supported this work. To all the members of the Manitoba Alliance for Universal Design for Learning (MAUDeL), who have worked so hard to share and shape this work and support me personally, many thanks. Thank you, too, to the members of the Canadian Research Centre on Inclusive Education, and especially Dr. Jacqueline Specht, its director, for their support. Many of my students at the university have influenced my thinking and honed this practice; I appreciate the collegial dialogue we have engaged in on

Portage & Main Press, 2013, *Resource Teachers*, ISBN: 978-1-55379-501-8

cold winter nights, with special thanks to Trish Glass and Don Shackel, who have co-taught the summer institutes and courses with such care and integrity.

To all the family, friends, mentors, and spiritual teachers who have guided my spirit, nurtured my heart, and enlightened my soul, my heartfelt thanks. Many thanks to my brother, Laurence, my sister, Vivi, my father, and my niece Jessica and nephews, Zach and Jorel, for their love and support. A special thank you to Reb Zalman, Reb Nadya, Reb Shefa, and Reb Victor for helping me connect my spiritual life with my profession and for guiding me on the journey — I am eternally grateful. To my soul sisters, Saida, Dafna, Lynna, Andi, and Lisa, my love and gratitude grow every day — thank you for the inspiration and connection.

Finally, as always, and with everything I do, I must credit the rock on which I stand, my mother. At eighty-three, she remains friend, mother, consultant, social worker, advisor, and spirit guide. There simply are no words — I am blessed.

Section One
Introduction

Portage & Main Press, 2013, *Resource Teachers*, ISBN: 978-1-55379-501-8

Chapter 1

The Three-Block Model of Universal Design for Learning

In *Teaching to Diversity* (TtD), I introduced my Three-Block Model (TBM) of Universal Design for Learning (UDL) as a framework for creating inclusive classrooms. Universal design for learning focuses on ensuring that the social and academic life of the classroom is accessible for diverse learners by creating socially and academically inclusive classrooms and schools.

Many provincial and territorial departments and ministries of education have now included UDL in their policies or recommended practices. A search of the websites reveals that only Prince Edward Island (PEI) and Newfoundland and Labrador (NL) make no reference to UDL in support of diverse learners. In contrast, New Brunswick goes so far as to say:

> The principle of Universal Design for Learning is the starting point for an inclusive public education system. (New Brunswick Department of Education, *Definition of Inclusion* 2009, 3)

Although PEI and NL do not use the term, they do use language that supports the philosophy of UDL. For example, in their *Service Delivery Model* (2011, 8), the Newfoundland and Labrador Department of Education says:

> Good teaching practices reflected in classrooms include:
> - creation of classrooms which employ a variety of processes and strategies responsive to student learning styles
> - recognition that supporting the unique strengths and needs of a particular student is likely to benefit other students
> - providing access to a wide variety of learning opportunities and working arrangements

Such language reflects the understanding that inclusive education can provide access to all, to the benefit of all, which is the foundational philosophy of UDL.

As professionals, we teachers must be willing to examine our profession critically, not only to acknowledge the gains we have made but also to recognize where there is further work to do. If we were members of the medical field, we could be happy that we have improved treatments for cancer and AIDS, and that these treatments have fewer negative side-effects. However, despite all the research, there is no cure yet for either disease. We would have to acknowledge, then, that

Portage & Main Press, 2013, *Resource Teachers*, ISBN: 978-1-55379-501-8

the medical field needs more research, and that there is still room for improvement. The same is true for us as teachers when we examine inclusive education. We have improved — more students are welcomed into regular classrooms than ever before, and academic outcomes for students with disabilities are improving. However, too many students still have to spend more than half their day outside the regular classroom, and too many students still drop out before finishing secondary school — a sign of their alienation and disengagement. We must, therefore, be willing to acknowledge that we need more research in teaching and learning, and that we still have room to grow and improve.

No framework for inclusive education can be effective without an initial focus on how and whether inclusive instructional practice takes place in general education classrooms. Looking back to the beginning of the inclusive movement in the early 1980s, I can see that it was a mistake to focus on a model of integrating "special" education into "general" education classrooms. This model might have worked, at least on the surface, when we had just one student being integrated into a general classroom, with a special education teacher present. Now, however, one-third of Canadian students require some kind of additional support to be successful along with the rest of their class, so the model falls apart. In most classrooms in Canadian schools, we have a large number of second-language learners and, in addition, several children who face learning challenges or social and emotional challenges, some gifted students, and others with recognized disabilities. I have seen classrooms in which teachers were expected to monitor several different behaviour intervention programs, to adapt instruction for half a dozen learners with individual learning needs, and to be aware of the students with anxiety disorders or sensory overload.

No principal or school board should expect one classroom teacher to handle between eight and ten different programs in their classroom, although this situation is deemed necessary when the school follows an individualized special education model. We also cannot afford to provide several special education teachers in every classroom. This conflict of priorities means that in schools across North America, we have handed the education of our neediest learners over to our least trained staff — educational assistants (EAs) — because the budget line for EA personnel is lower than that for more highly trained educators. Researchers have long noted how ineffective this model is, because it stigmatizes students socially and limits their educational opportunity (Giangreco 2010). But this model arose from the belief that each student who needs an individualized educational program also requires a one-to-one staff member as support. Thus, we ended up with a fiscally driven decision — the economic reality of employing EAs despite the common-sense recognition that struggling learners need a teacher.

A key principle of UDL is that instructional practices can be designed to allow all learners to enter into the learning in a general education classroom, that is, without requiring a separate program for each child with special needs. The Ontario Ministry's *Education for All* (2005) describes this aspect of UDL:

Portage & Main Press, 2013, *Resource Teachers*, ISBN: 978-1-55379-501-8

> UDL is intended to ensure that teaching will meet the needs of all students. This does not mean planning instruction for students with average achievement levels, and then making after-the-fact modifications to meet the special needs of certain students. UDL encourages teachers to develop a class profile and then plan, from the beginning, to provide means and pedagogical materials that meet the needs of all students and not only those with special needs. (p.11)

As stated, this does *not* mean a one-size-fits-all approach. Instead, teachers are encouraged to create multiple entry points in curricula so that all students, with or without disabilities, can access the content in their own way. Nova Scotia Education's Student Services produced a fact sheet entitled "Inclusion: Supporting All Students" that itemizes many key indicators of inclusive schools, among them "a focus on outcomes for all students that students work toward in a variety of ways." In other words, all students work toward planned curricular outcomes, but they achieve these expectations to varying degrees and in differentiated ways.

This approach in education is analogous to the universal design approach in modern architecture of providing optional means of entering a building — stairs or a ramp, above ground or underground. People can choose their preferred means of entry to arrive in the same lobby. Although the ramp may have initially been built for people using wheelchairs, other people also benefit — parents with strollers, people with briefcases or suitcases on rollers, and so on. In education, comparably, researchers have identified the practices in our classrooms that provide the "ramps" to teaching and learning the curriculum — practices such as inquiry-based learning, differentiated instruction and assessment, and cooperative learning. These practices allow learners who do not learn well through traditional text-based input (followed by independent seatwork on pencil-and-paper activities) to successfully master concepts and skills in the ways that work better for them, for how their mind works. These students can then engage not only academically but also socially as they join with their peers in the life of the classroom rather than being separated and instructed one-on-one by an EA. Such engagement has profound effects on the students' self-concept, social relationships, and learning (Katz and Epp 2013; Katz and Porath 2011). To implement universal design for learning, teachers of both general and special education require training in inclusive instructional practices that can provide the ramps for diverse learners while also making teachers' workloads more manageable.

TtD: p. 13

According to the June 2001 Workplace Survey by the Canadian Teachers' Federation (Brackenreed 2011, 4), "47% of teachers quit before retirement age due to stress and frustration." In general education, teachers support the philosophy of inclusion; however, they feel ill-equipped to teach diverse learners, and become stressed out by their perceived inability to "meet the needs" (Katz, in submission). In fact, a positive attitude has been shown to increase teacher burnout, perhaps because those who believe strongly in the value of inclusion are most stressed by their self-perceived inability to make it work (Talmor, Reiter, and Feigin 2005). Many special education teachers and resource teachers have unmanageable caseloads, a situation that leaves classroom teachers to cope on their own with increasingly diverse classrooms. Losing almost one-half of the experienced teaching workforce is destructive to the system, the students, and the teachers themselves. This is why it is so critical that we focus first on inclusive instructional practice. Such concentration of effort will serve to:

- improve student outcomes
- reduce the caseloads of special education and resource teachers
- increase self-efficacy and job satisfaction for general classroom teachers, as they develop the expertise to design a learning community that
  - creates a positive classroom climate
  - reduces challenging behaviour
  - improves educational achievement, without overloading teachers

TtD: p. 25

TtD: Ch.3

TtD: Ch.4, Ch.5

In *Teaching to Diversity*, I described in detail the ways in which a general education teacher can do just that — by using the Three-Block Model of UDL. This model expands the UDL traditional focus on technology and differentiation to explore both the social and academic practices of an inclusive classroom. Block One, Social and Emotional Learning, sets the foundation for inclusion through the Respecting Diversity (RD) program, with the goal of building a class climate that respects diversity and develops a positive self-concept in all students. Block Two includes a planning framework and teaching practices that allow for student choice, so that students are able to develop conceptual understanding and access activities and materials in ways that work for them. This model synthesizes evidence-based practices for planning, instruction, and assessment of diverse learners in ways that reduce teacher workload and facilitate teachers' ability to instruct small groups at their instructional level. This synthesis is key to the model and not "one more thing" for teachers to do. Rather, it helps teachers synthesize all the tasks they have been asked to handle — in practical, do-able ways. The UDL classroom created by this model maintains the high expectations set by the provincial curriculum for all students, while it supports teachers' self-efficacy and reduces their workload as they do not have to plan multiple programs. In Block Three, I delineated the reforms needed in educational systems and structures to increase the efficacy of inclusion.

TtD: Ch.6

One teacher commented: "It makes my life as a teacher so much easier, and I marvel at how I didn't figure it out myself."

The outcome of combining evidence-based practices such as differentiating instruction, teaching to the essential understandings, assigning inquiry projects, and using assessment for learning in one comprehensive model is beginning to be revealed. In terms of student engagement, autonomy, and pro-social interactions with peers and teachers, recent studies show that the Three-Block Model produces significant positive results for students from grade 1 to grade 12 (Katz, in submission; Katz 2012c). Theresa Glass (2013), in a pilot project, revealed that these gains in engagement and self-concept held true also for students who are

Portage & Main Press, 2013, *Resource Teachers*, ISBN: 978-1-55379-501-8

disengaged and struggling both behaviourally and academically. Students involved in these learning communities have reported stronger feelings of belonging, an improved self-concept, and greater willingness to include others (Katz, Porath, Bendu, and Epp 2012). Overall, classroom climates have improved with increased pro-social behaviour and a reduction in aggressive and disruptive behaviour (Katz and Porath 2011).

It is particularly important to note the significant results in the secondary school setting, because previous studies emphasized the difficulty of implementing inclusion effectively in secondary settings (Mastropieri 2001; McNeely, Nonnemaker, and Blum 2002). Through planning the instructional environments in ways that increase accessibility, teacher workload is reduced; they do not need to plan separate programs for students who cannot currently access the regular curriculum. Teachers reported an increased sense of self-efficacy regarding their ability to include students with disabilities and to meet the needs of diverse learners when implementing this framework (Katz, in submission). The evidence is mounting that the Three-Block Model of Universal Design for Learning can be effective for all (Katz and Epp 2013).

In *Teaching to Diversity*, I presented in great detail (chapters 4 and 5) the ways in which special education teachers, resource teachers, and general classroom teachers can collaborate to support inclusive classrooms. Nevertheless, even within the ideal inclusive classroom, we have students who require specialized supports in order to be successful in their classroom. In chapter 5, I introduced the Response to Intervention (RTI) model as a way to understand the scaffolding of supports that are necessary in an inclusive school system. The model makes clear that the planning and instructional process is focused on improving our use of Tier 1 intervention, which means programming according to UDL principles. This does not mean that we do not recognize and value Tier 2 and Tier 3 supports.

TtD: pp. 138–39

At present, however, we have far too many students who require these supports and, thus, we are overloading our support personnel, which leaves our classroom teachers feeling overwhelmed. This situation is evident in, for instance, the issue of struggling readers. According to the Participation and Activity Limitation Survey (PALS Statistics Canada) of 2006, 3.2 percent of our students have severe learning disabilities. We recognize and value the supports identified as Tier 2 and Tier 3, which these students will undoubtedly require for literacy instruction. But when you ask classroom teachers how many of their students are not reading at grade level, the numbers they provide range from 25 percent to 75 percent — although only 3 percent actually have a disability. This means that between 22 percent and 72 percent of our students — who have no disability — are not learning to read well.

In other words, we teachers are failing to teach a significant number of our students how to read! Yes, some of this is environmental — such as the lack of exposure to language or not being read to in early childhood — but we must take responsibility for a significant portion of this shortfall. We have failed to differentiate our literacy instruction and use methods that help students learn how to read — in

Portage & Main Press, 2013, *Resource Teachers*, ISBN: 978-1-55379-501-8

ways that work for them. As discussed, if one treatment is not working, doctors seek a better treatment. Our treatment of reading instruction is not working, which does not make us bad teachers, but does indicate simply that we need a new treatment. This is just one example of the areas in which we must expand our Tier 1 classroom-based instruction to ensure that diverse learners can benefit from it.

Having said all of that, there is a place for Tier 2 and Tier 3 instruction, as the New Brunswick policy (2002) articulates so well:

> The principle of Universal Design for Learning is the starting point for an inclusive public education system. This principle holds that the needs of the greatest number of students be met by maximizing the usability of programs, services, practices and learning environments. When Universal Design for Learning alone is insufficient to meet the needs of an individual student or groups of students, accommodations are required, both ethically and legally. (p. 3)

However, there are differences in how the role of the "special educator" or "resource teacher" (RT) is enacted in a UDL instructional framework. In fact, this is where the roles of special education teacher and resource teacher diverge. In the UDL model, a resource teacher is exactly that — a resource, not a special education teacher — and the roles of general educator and resource teacher become blurred. Both teachers become facilitators of an inclusive learning community, and also become responsible not only for all the students in that community but also for their social and academic engagement. The students are no longer "your kids" and "my kids," they are only "our kids." Like any good parents, both teachers play a role with every child, albeit a different role. Despite this blurring, we still recognize the areas of expertise and skill in the individual teachers, just as father and mother both bring their different strengths to the raising of a child, but both share in the nurturing of all their children. In Newfoundland and Labrador's *Service Delivery Model for Students with Exceptionalities* (2011), this fundamental change is recognized in the statement:

> The inclusive model embodies a more collaborative approach to teaching and learning. Within a school community, all members are encouraged to share responsibility for the learning and well-being of all students. (p. 5)

In this way, resource teachers become partners with classroom teachers in the creation of inclusive learning communities by co-planning, co-teaching, and co-assessing instructional programs. Over time, both teachers are monitoring the social and academic progress of all students and, when needed, provide supports to ensure success. This collaborative work will significantly improve student success and reduce the numbers of students requiring Tier 2 and Tier 3 supports and, thus, the caseload of RTs. Obviously, this approach is preferable for all involved, but especially for the students because it allows them to be successful in their classroom without the stigmatization of labelling, pull-out services, and school failure.

When, despite powerful Tier 1 instruction, a student still struggles with learning, the two teachers can meet to assess the student's strengths and possible barriers to learning, then decide on whether the student requires Tier 2 intervention. The RT's expertise may, at this point, help them provide the resources and conduct ecobehavioural observations or other specialized assessments in order to guide the Tier 2 programming. Sometimes, despite the best efforts of both teachers, a student continues to have significant difficulties — socially or academically or both. The RT should, then, coordinate a team who can provide the intensive, individualized assessment whose results will lead the team to develop an individual education plan (IEP) for the student. That is, the plan is developed only after classroom-based assessment and interventions have not fully succeeded in supporting the student in question.

In subsequent chapters, I explain this process in detail as well as the skills and concepts that underlie it. This procedure marks a fundamental shift in the definition of the resource teacher, that is, a shift *away from* the special education teacher who adapted and modified individual plans focused on remediation and *toward* the educator who focuses on supporting all students in their efforts to achieve success in their classroom. At all three RTI tier levels, our goal remains not one of "fixing the student" but one of finding and providing the kind of support that the student requires in order to be successful socially and academically. To begin, we review the fundamental concepts from *Teaching to Diversity* and the Three-Block Model of UDL:

- our definition of social and academic inclusion
- how the Three-Block Model fits with traditional UDL frameworks (e.g., CAST <www.cast.org>)
- how UDL and RTI can fit together in an inclusive system to redefine the role of the RT

From there, we delve into each of the three tiers of intervention, the role of the RT within these tiers, and the knowledge and skills necessary to be able to implement them successfully.

Chapter 2
What We Mean by "Inclusive"

Key terms and concepts
- social inclusion, social exclusion
- academic inclusion, academic exclusion
- inclusive education
- *Salamanca Statement*

Essential understandings
Inclusive education means that:
- every child is a part of the social and academic life of the classroom and the school
- every child has the chance to feel good about themselves and what they contribute to the learning and social community
- every child has the opportunity to experience academic challenge, success, and growth
- every child feels a sense of belonging and interconnectedness

Inclusive education has been a global consideration for more than three decades. Most educators agree that *all* children and youth would, ideally, be included in our school systems and classrooms. However, many doubt that such full inclusion is possible. Educators report that they are constrained by limited resources, by increasing student diversity, and by lack of training (Bennett 2009). How can we restore imagination, inspiration, and passion to the dialogue about — and the implementation of — inclusive education? How do we show students, parents, teachers, and administrators that not only is inclusive education possible but it can be achieved in spite of the perceived realities of budgets, systems, and student diversity?

Let's begin with the vision, with stretching beyond what we think are the limits of the possible. Teachers, especially resource teachers (RTs), are realists, which means that we focus on the practical and the how-to. But without a vision of the possible, we can get caught up in the limitations of the day-to-day functioning of the system, the mentality of "This is how it is," and we can lose sight of the vision. Take a moment and envision your ideal inclusive classroom and school. What does it sound like? look like? feel like? What kind of learning is taking place? How are the educators, the students, and their families interacting with one another? You must know what you are striving for in order to filter the various strategies

Portage & Main Press, 2013, *Resource Teachers*, ISBN: 978-1-55379-501-8

and frameworks that the professional development world puts forward. When you know where you want to go, you can decide which professional development workshops, which books, and what other resources will be useful in taking you and your students where you want to go. When you do not have a clear vision, you can be easily overwhelmed by the many different strategies you encounter in a teaching career.

Imagine that all your students are feeling that they belong, that they are valued for who they are, and that they are seen and understood as individuals. Imagine a school in which the teachers and students have truly learned to value all the differences each has to offer, and where students know that their contribution counts. Imagine a place in which all students are challenged to learn, to grow, and to reach their full potential. *Imagination*, in this context, is more a synonym for *vision* than for *creativity*. Of course, one can also have a creative vision. What is your vision?

Some have defined inclusive education as "including those students who have previously been excluded, that is, students with disabilities." Similarly, "diverse learners" has often been a euphemism for students with disabilities or students from cultural and linguistic minority populations. But inclusive education means so much more. It means encompassing all students, that is, providing an educational environment where all students are welcomed and included. How I learn differs from how you learn; my background knowledge, life experiences, personality, and interests differ from yours — and any given classroom contains as many different learners as there are people. Children are diverse in personality, in ethnicity, in languages, in family structures, and in learning styles. Their similarities and differences all contribute to the makeup of a diverse classroom. Inclusive education has to be about all these children — the goal of inclusion is to provide high quality education to all students.

To look forward and imagine what achieving inclusive education would look like, we first have to examine where we've come from, what we tried along the way that didn't work, what issues we confronted and resolved, and what issues we still need to resolve in our education systems. Through this review, we can see how much progress we have actually made.

At one time, many youth with disabilities could not attend school, nor could many children who lived at a distance from school or in remote areas. Many of my parents' generation left school after grade 4 or grade 6 to work on their farm or to begin an apprenticeship because school "was not for them." Today although our education systems make room for all students in our schools, we still have good reasons to change and grow. Like all professions, we have made progress, but we must realize that innovations will take place in our field that will improve our ability to meet the needs of diverse learners. From professional conversations and both educational and societal research shaping the vision for inclusive education, two themes — social inclusion and academic inclusion — emerge.

Portage & Main Press, 2013, *Resource Teachers*, ISBN: 978-1-55379-501-8

Social Inclusion and Social Exclusion

Many students in our schools would, if asked, tell you they feel that they have no friends, that nobody likes them, and that nobody even notices them. In sociology and social justice terms, social exclusion usually refers to marginalized populations. In schools, it's not only students from marginalized groups who are socially excluded.

Social inclusion means involving all students to give them a sense of belonging and connectedness (Koster, Nakken, Pijl, and van Houten 2009). From when students enter the school in the morning, the characteristics of social inclusion include being greeted in the halls by friends and teachers, having peers to interact with during breaks, working with partners and group members for learning activities, and being involved in school teams, clubs, and taking leadership roles. Social inclusion, therefore, is about recognizing and valuing diversity in education settings. Social inclusion means that all students have opportunities to be part of the school community and to learn and grow alongside their peers — a definition of inclusion recognized in many provinces. Alberta's policy, for example, states that "inclusion in the education system is about ensuring that each student belongs and receives a quality education no matter their ability, disability, language, cultural background, gender, or age." Note the use of the word "belongs." Two populations have been more likely to be socially excluded in schools — students with exceptionalities, and students who are First Nations, Métis, or Inuit (FNMI).

Social Inclusion of Students with Exceptionalities

When we place students in segregated classrooms, or have them working with an educational asitant (EA), at the back of a classroom, we prevent them from forming social relationships with their peers, which means they are socially excluded. When we bus children to a school outside their neighbourhood, we ensure that not only these students but also their parents will be socially excluded from the community. It's in the halls of our schools that parents meet one another when volunteering for school activities or when arranging play dates for their kids. When the community's educational system buses a student with a disability to a different school outside the community, the parents of that student do not get to meet the parents of other nearby students nor do the children get to know one another. Consequently, there is no relationship, no community supporting their inclusion after school, on holidays, and during the summer when they are at the local park or community centre. Because parents of children with special needs already feel isolated, this lack of community involvement is likely to increase their isolation. The decisions made by the education system can thus result in the segregation of students with exceptional needs and in negative classroom climates and peer interactions, and can even increase alienation and bullying — which leads to a reduction in educational achievement for all students (Symes and Humphrey 2010).

Ryndak, Morrison, and Sommerstein (1999) report on the case of Melinda, an American girl with a developmental disability, who was moved from special classes to an inclusive classroom. Subsequently, when Melinda made a presentation at a local conference on inclusion and a moderator asked her what the difference was between the special class and the regular class, Melinda replied, "When I was in a special class, I used to put my head down on the desk. I used to look out the door and watch the kids go by, and now they're my friends" (p. 15). Melinda's experience was so profound that she wrote a letter to testify in a debate for the Education Committee of the State Assembly. In the letter, she referred to being able to learn from watching "what her friends do" and being "taught by her friends and teaching them, as well" as an example of the least restrictive environment.

Students who are gifted may also struggle to fit in socially with their peers. When their advanced cognitive ability combines with their intense emotionality or sensitivity, it is hard for them to determine who their peers really are. Are the students who have the same interests as them their peers, even if they are years older? Not really, because those students have a different level of social maturity. Are their schoolmates of the same chronological age their peers? Not really, because their interests and perceptions are significantly different. When combined, the traits of divergent thinking and reacting more intensely to emotional situations make gifted students feel isolated, different, and misunderstood.

Social Inclusion of FNMI Students

Most First Nations cultures believe that children are a gift from the creator. The job of a parent and the community is to treasure such a gift and to nurture the affinities and talents of that child on all four levels of the sacred circle — spiritual, physical, mental, and emotional — so that the child may have a good life (*Mino Pimatisiwin*). The questions for educators are: How can we help children — all children — have a good life? How do we define a good life? What are the implications for the child's life while in school for 12 to 14 years, 10 months a year?

For many Aboriginal parents, the traditional school system is antithetical to their beliefs about raising children. They believe the child will naturally follow the path they were meant to. For example, if the child follows the shaman around, then an apprenticeship relationship will naturally occur. If the child is drawn to the artist, the hunter, or the dancer instead, then those interests will be nurtured. These beliefs reflect differentiation and multiple intelligences at their finest. But the traditional school system asks these parents to make their children do things such as homework that the children don't want to do. Their teachers write up individual education plans (IEPs) that focus on what the child cannot do, and ignore what they can do and want to do. These approaches make the education system seem backward to both children and parents, particularly when educators misjudge the situation and say that the parents "don't support the program." These parents love their children; they just don't love a system that focuses on deficits rather than strengths, a system with a history of abusing its power in relations with First Nations. To them, elements within the education system appear intent on finding only the negative in FNMI children.

Portage & Main Press, 2013, *Resource Teachers*, ISBN: 978-1-55379-501-8

In contrast, the Three-Block Model of UDL focuses on developing a balance of wellness in the mental, spiritual, physical, and emotional aspects of life. Such balance can help schools and school systems feel more culturally relevant, more compassionate, and more inviting to FNMI families. When non-Aboriginals fully recognize the cultures, values, and ways of being among Aboriginal groups within our walls, these students and their parents will feel at home in our schools. An atmosphere of acceptance and a pedagogy that is culturally relevant will improve their engagement in learning at school and, in doing so, improve their achievement. Many provinces have begun to recognize this. In Saskatchewan, units of study in science that include Aboriginal perspectives have been developed with the goal of making "Western science and engineering accessible to Aboriginal students in ways that nurture their own cultural identities; . . . so students are not expected to set aside their culture's view of the material world when they study science at school" <www.usask.ca/education/ccstu/welcome.html>. Such inclusion is critically important because, in the past, Aboriginal beliefs have been dismissed as legends or myths.

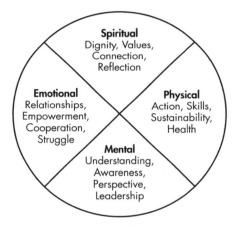

Figure 2.1 Icon representing the balance of wellness

FNMI and the Three-Block Model

1. In **Block One: Social and Emotional Learning,** my Respecting Diversity (RD) program seeks to develop a sense of pride and dignity in all students' knowing that who they are and what they have to offer the community is of value. Through the first four RD lessons, students are engaged in reflecting not only on their interests and talents but also on their strengths and weaknesses in these different ways of learning. Teachers can encourage their students to become aware of their own "intelligence profile" and empower the students to work out how they can use their strengths to become valued members of both their learning community and their larger

Portage & Main Press, 2013, *Resource Teachers*, ISBN: 978-1-55379-501-8

Spotlight

To watch instructional videos on how to use the RD program in your class, visit: <www.threeblockmodel.com/respecting-diversity-program-videos.html>.

community. Students begin to recognize that what they have to offer is of value. In the second four lessons, students develop a sense of belonging, of being included and of being cared for, of interconnectedness with something larger than ourselves. In these lessons, the focus changes to respecting diverse others, being inclusive and cooperative, and assuming leadership when needed, which all fit well with the balanced perspective of the medicine wheel.

2.   **In Block Two, Inclusive Instructional Practice**, the instruction is focused on using students' strengths and developing their resiliency to persevere through challenges with the support of their learning team and learning community. The concept that community is critical to resiliency is a fundamental value of most First Nations cultures. This value differs significantly from the cultures that have emphasized independence, whereby children are expected to face a learning challenge on their own and to keep trying. For many students who struggle with verbal-linguistic tasks, this expectation means that they spend five hours a day, five days a week, for twelve years doing what they cannot do. Yet, they are expected to keep trying and to behave appropriately, as in "Do not object, or you will be labelled 'oppositional'." Then we wonder why students disengage.

FNMI cultures emphasize *interdependence* over *independence* — as does the use of small-group and cooperative structures in schools and classrooms. In my Three-Block Model, I have called them "learning teams," a way to create a true learning community. The use of multiple intelligences as a framework for differentiation includes learning opportunities that involve bodily-kinesthetic and hands-on activities. Through these activities, students develop skills and connect to the physical, intellectual, and emotional realms of the medicine wheel. Many learners find that these ways are best in helping them learn and develop skills. They become accepted as members of the learning community rather than becoming those students who "cannot sit still" and "cannot do the work." By combining the big ideas of curricular themes with activities calling on different intelligences, teachers can focus their students' attention on existential issues related to sustainability and help cultivate their awareness of global issues and connections.

3.   **In Block Three: Systems and Structures**, I emphasize the concept of distributed leadership within the broader learning community, which invites input from the community and student leadership and resembles the councils within many FNMI cultures. Respect for the Elders of the community and their wisdom is critical to creating a relationship with FNMI parents and community. Collaborative, co-teaching structures resemble the community collaboration seen in many FN cultures. The IEP

process that I put forward in my Three-Block Model of UDL focuses on developing students' strengths and strategies for coping with challenges rather than insisting on remediation.

Put together, as one Cree elder stated: "You have synthesized the wisdom of our grandmothers." (Elder Gwen Merrick)

Academic Inclusion and Academic Exclusion

Academic inclusion is more than just geography. It does not mean just placing students together in a classroom. It means that all students learn through interaction with each other while focusing on concepts and skills in the general curriculum. When we relegate a student to learning only "life skills" because we have decided that they cannot learn, and we deny them access to the curriculum (which includes literacy and numeracy), we exclude them not only from our classrooms but also from the larger community as they grow older and seek jobs requiring a high school diploma. Students come to school to learn, and to do so with their peers. When we instruct them only in one-to-one situations with adults — in the back of a classroom, in the hallway, or in the library, we exclude them both academically and socially.

In the Ryndak article (1999), we learn that Melinda, when placed in the inclusive classroom, developed her literacy skills well beyond expectations. At age 15, she had been described as the lowest functioning student in her special education classroom. In that classroom, the teacher had focused Melinda's instruction on basic reading, writing, and math. Melinda developed "an aversion to reading" (p. 11) and was reading at a grade 2 level. After she was included in a regular classroom, Melinda demonstrated tremendous growth in oral language, in reading, and in writing. This growth was so striking that she was invited to speak to the House Committee on the Least Restrictive Environment (US House of Representatives) and was able to attend college on a modified program after graduation. She read college textbooks written at a grade 7 level or above with complete comprehension. As Melinda reached adulthood, her mother stated:

> I attribute the growth to higher expectation on the part of everybody.... People expected her to be retarded and then they gave her activities that they would expect retarded people to do. Those tests and statistics really are not a good forecaster of what any child can do, if given the proper opportunities, role models, and settings. (p. 19)

Melinda's case indicates that teachers in her inclusive classroom made efforts to include her in academic learning with her peers. Although efforts are made in other cases to socially include students with significant disabilities, little attempt is made to educate them or to include them academically. In a study by Diane Carroll et al. (2011), exemplary schools with reputations for being inclusive were found to have extensive programming related to social inclusion for students with significant disabilities, but *explicit instruction for students with the most severe disabilities was almost non-existent* (p. 124). Pat Mirenda, one of Canada's leading experts on the inclusion of students with an autism-related disorder and developmental disabilities, once said:

> I think we made a mistake arguing inclusion on the basis of social justice. It led to people believing that as long as they wheeled the student into the room, and they were smiling and had a friend, that was all that mattered. But students could be happy and make a friend at home or in the community. They come to school to learn. ALL students. (Personal conversation)

In this regard, we must note that some of our most gifted students are also excluded because they, too, do not receive the appropriate level of curriculum and instructional activities, and they feel isolated socially (Jackson 1998; Stoeger and Ziegler 2010). Far too many students, with and without disabilities, are neither challenged nor engaged academically in appropriate ways.

TtD: p. 158

Canada and UNESCO's Goal of Education for All

In 1994, representatives of 92 nations gathered in Salamanca, Spain, to discuss inclusive education under the umbrella of the United Nations Educational, Scientific and Cultural Organization (UNESCO). The resulting document, the *Salamanca Statement…* (UNESCO 1994) described their belief in the right to "education for all" children. The guiding principle of the framework adopted was that schools:

> should accommodate all children regardless of their physical, intellectual, social, emotional, linguistic, or other conditions (p. 6).

The *Salamanca Statement* further recognized

> the necessity and urgency of providing education for children, youth and adults with special educational needs within the regular education system (UNESCO 1994, p. viii).

Canada was among the nations that signed the statement, yet across our provinces and territories, Aboriginal students, students with disabilities, and the students who are culturally and linguistically diverse (many facing varied social issues or disengagement from learning) are still excluded from regular classrooms in many communities. What, then, is our vision for the future? Is it possible to have school systems in which every child is a part of the social and academic life of their classroom, their school, and their community — every child, no exceptions — even given the realities of current conditions in the system? The answer is yes.

Even before we knew how to do it well, inclusive education had positive outcomes for all involved. Early researchers responded to the concern that including students with disabilities would require too much teacher time and require changes in the complexity and pace of the curriculum, which would have negative effects on the other students. However, research has not borne out that negative expectation. In comparisons of students' literacy and numeracy skills, the scores (on standardized tests) of both the typical and the gifted students in the same classrooms as students with disabilities were identical with those of similar students in classrooms that did not also have students with disabilities. Similarly, their rate of postsecondary enrolment and other academic scores showed no difference even when their classrooms had students with significant behavioural challenges (Bru 2009; Crisman 2008; Kalambouka, Farrell, Dyson, and Kaplan 2007). This research has been replicated over decades and across countries (Curcic 2009). In some cases, research has shown that students with and without disabilities make significantly greater gains in reading, writing, and mathematics in inclusive classrooms (Cole, Waldron, Majd, and Hasazi 2004). It is clear that the presence of students with disabilities, including those with challenging behaviours, does not negatively impact the learning of other students.

The next stage of research explored the outcomes of inclusive education for the students with disabilities. Around the world, such students, when placed in inclusive settings, demonstrate improved academic outcomes (including literacy, numeracy, general knowledge, and higher-order thinking skills) in contrast with peers of the same level of disability in segregated classrooms (Katz and Mirenda 2002a). Perhaps more surprising, the students with disabilities, when in inclusive classrooms, outperformed their segregated peers in both adaptive and life skills and in vocational and academic competence (Kurth and Mastergeorge 2010; Myklebust 2006). The role played by peer models in the same classroom is a powerful one for the students with disabilities. In a national study of outcomes related to inclusive education in Canada, the students in inclusive settings were reported to be in better general health, progressing more in school, interacting better with peers, and more frequently looking forward to attending school than those in less inclusive settings (Timmons and Wagner 2008). All signatory nations on the *Salamanca Agreement* have made progress in implementing inclusive education — despite the limited opportunities for teacher training, the reductions in resources, and the pressures to standardize achievement and accountability — and children around the world are benefiting. Imagine the possibilities!

Interactive Inclusion

In child development, three stages of social awareness and play are described:

- **Egocentrism**: Infants are aware only of themselves. They cry to be fed and changed without awareness of others' needs, contributions, and so on.

- **Parallel play**: Toddlers become aware of others and imitate them. When they see an older sibling playing with a toy such as a car, they, too, pick up a car and imitate their sibling's play. However, they play alongside the sibling, not with the sibling. They do not try to push their car over to the other's and have a race or develop an imaginary game.

- **Interactive play**: Young children become aware of the joy of connection. They play with others, engaging in dialogue and shared experience.

Portage & Main Press, 2013, *Resource Teachers*, ISBN: 978-1-55379-501-8

Our history as inclusive educators has followed the same path. In the early stages, we were egocentric, unaware of anyone who did not fit our needs and desires. We simply excluded them; that is, we placed them in institutions or special schools. As we began to mature, we learned how to parallel play; we placed special classes in regular schools so they could live alongside us, but not with us. Sometimes, we placed children in a regular classroom, but their program was a parallel program. They did math when we did math, but a different math, usually with an educational assistant and not in interaction with their peers.

It is time, now, to grow into maturity, to achieve interactive inclusion, that is, a mature feeling of inclusion and interaction. We need to develop a system in which we all grow and learn in interaction with each other, celebrating what our diversity brings, sharing our triumphs and challenges, and creating compassionate learning communities for all of our children and youth. It can be done. In *Teaching to Diversity* (Katz 2012a), I described how the classroom teacher can create an interactively inclusive classroom. In this book, I describe the role that the resource teacher plays in such an endeavour. The reader might therefore benefit from reviewing *Teaching to Diversity* before continuing in this book.

Portage & Main Press, 2013, *Resource Teachers*, ISBN: 978-1-55379-501-8

Resource Teacher as Educational Leader and Collaborator

Portage & Main Press, 2013, *Resource Teachers*, ISBN: 978-1-55379-501-8

Chapter 3

Response to Intervention in Universal Design for Learning

Key terms and concepts
- response to intervention (RTI)
- Tier 1, Tier 2, Tier 3
- service delivery models

Essential understandings
- The role of the resource teacher in an inclusive system has changed to that of collaborator and teacher leader.
- RTI is a systematic approach to service delivery for inclusive education.
  - All students should receive the bulk of their education in Tier 1, that is, in the general education classroom as delivered by a general education teacher or co-teaching team.
  - With Tier 2 interventions for some students, teachers strategize and target specific skills, concepts, or behaviours but in the regular classroom and for short periods of time.
  - Tier 3 interventions should be implemented only after Tier 1 and Tier 2 resources have been attempted. With these interventions, teachers provide intensive, multi-disciplinary supports for students with significant needs in their classrooms to the greatest extent possible.

School systems that are implementing inclusive education ask teachers not only to deliver increasingly complex curricula for increasingly diverse populations of students but also to include additional support for students with exceptionalities. As the number of students being referred for specialized services has increased, new models of collaborative practice have been developed to meet their needs. Response to Intervention (RTI) is one effective model, a tiered system of intervention and collaboration that describes a process for resource teachers who work alongside classroom teachers to guide small-group or individual programming for such students. RTI describes three tiers or levels of intervention that provide services — evidence-based instructional strategies of increasing intensity — to help ensure the academic growth and achievement of all students.

Portage & Main Press, 2013, *Resource Teachers*, ISBN: 978-1-55379-501-8

A Tiered System of Interventions

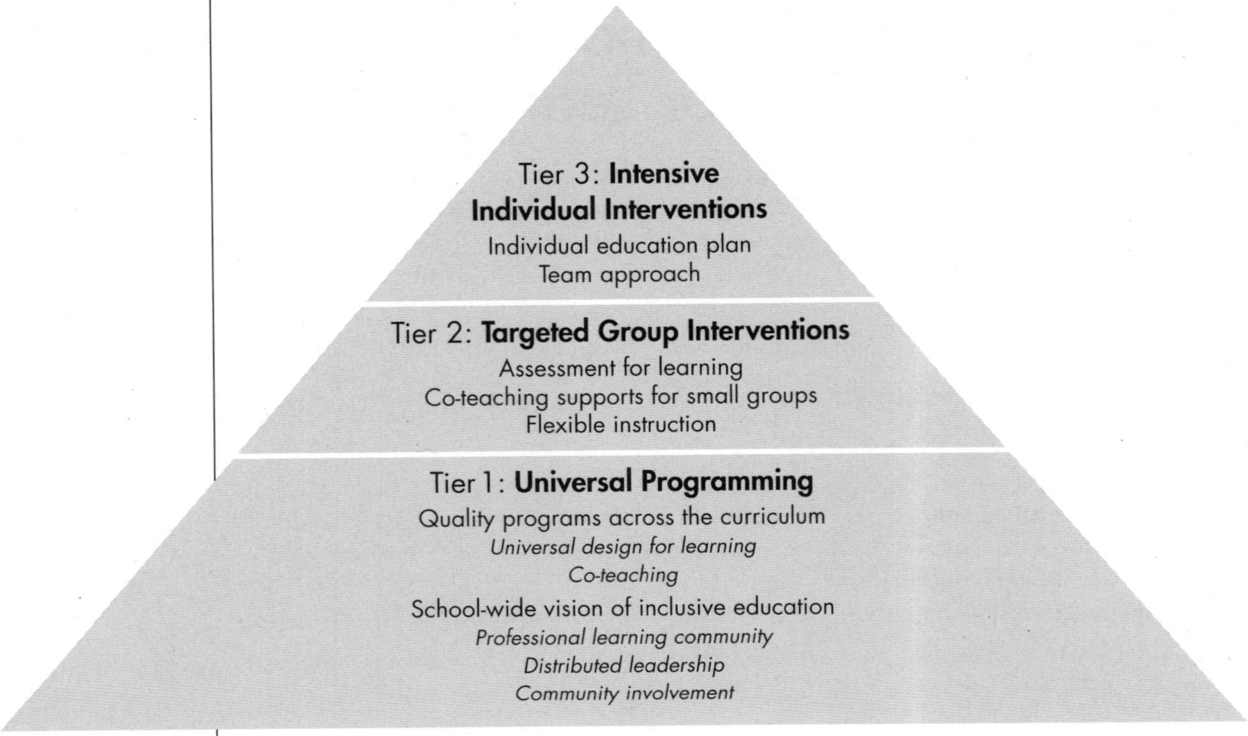

Tier 3: **Intensive Individual Interventions**
Individual education plan
Team approach

Tier 2: **Targeted Group Interventions**
Assessment for learning
Co-teaching supports for small groups
Flexible instruction

Tier 1: **Universal Programming**
Quality programs across the curriculum
Universal design for learning
Co-teaching
School-wide vision of inclusive education
Professional learning community
Distributed leadership
Community involvement

Figure 3.1 Response to Intervention Pyramid

RTI Tier 1

The first tier is based on the assumption that universal design for learning is alive and well in the classroom and that students are, thus, receiving core classroom instruction that is differentiated, universally designed, and provided to all. It is critical that, before specialized instruction is started, teachers should be involving all students in the same instruction and the same learning activities. In other words, teachers do not decide that a student cannot do the school work or cannot learn before that student has even been allowed to try, so we lower our expectations or segregate them. Quebec's Ministry of Education, Recreation and Sports states this policy well in their IEP document, *Individualized Education Plans*, 2004:

> The main focus should be on providing a student with particular needs with the same services as all other students, before more specialized, adapted services are considered.

With universal design for learning active in the school community, both classroom teachers and resource teachers begin the school year with the Respecting Diversity (RD) program for getting to know their students and creating the climate for a school community. They discuss their expectations for group work, and they teach their students how to represent concepts in multi-modal ways. They also initiate formative assessment activities to provide a baseline on what their students know and can do, how they learn best, and what they find challenging. Having designed their units of study according to the criteria of universal design for learning, the teachers begin differentiated instruction — within the general classroom — including instructional supports, learning teams, inquiry groups, small-group reviews, or one-on-one direct teaching of a concept as needed by individual students.

Assessment in the classroom is focused on assessment for learning and should be ongoing. Assessments that are curriculum-based show teachers the growth of individual students over time and help them determine whether their students are progressing as expected. This process gradually and clearly identifies for teachers what their students already know and what they need to know. It is also effective in determining the best ways to teach what the students — whole class, or small groups, or individuals — are missing. When a student shows signs of struggling, the teaching team can follow a problem-solving process to determine what interventions will work within whole-class activities (e.g., using technology, allowing alternative responses, providing visual schedules, and so on). In this Tier 1 phase, the emphasis for both teachers is still on getting to know the students, on building relationships and a sense of community.

RTI Tier 2

When a teacher becomes concerned about a student's learning, behaviour, or social and emotional well-being, the team can conduct an ecobehavioural assessment — that is, an assessment of the instructional design and environment — to determine whether these are an optimal match with the student's learning profile. This assessment is not about judging the teachers, but it is about recognizing that no teacher is the perfect teacher for every child. As teachers, we must be willing to step out of our ego, explore what aspects of our program might not be working for a particular student or group of students even though it might be excellent for many others, and then find out which strategies can be introduced to the whole class that will simultaneously support the struggling students. Such strategies might include building in activities that require the students to move about, or providing visual aids, or introducing technology such as a SMART board for the whole class.

Most interventions at the Tier 2 level are intended to support small groups of students with similar needs, although they might also be offered to all students. For example, with a class in which several students cannot maintain attention, or follow detailed oral instructions, or remember and repeat facts (as in a set of times tables in mathematics), the teachers can design interventions first for all students in the general classroom setting. Such strategies as breaking tasks down into smaller chunks, providing opportunities for active movement, posting or writing instructions on the board, and teaching mnemonic strategies will benefit many

Portage & Main Press, 2013, *Resource Teachers*, ISBN: 978-1-55379-501-8

students in the class. Supplemental interventions for a set period of time — short-term and specific — focused on developing specific skills could take place within or outside the general education classroom. In other words, we must ensure that no student becomes "a resource kid" for an entire school year.

In Tier 2, the main purpose for monitoring progress is to determine whether the interventions are successful in helping the selected students learn at an appropriate rate. Regular assessments should take place to determine when a student might no longer require extra interventions, or when the interventions need to be changed, or when a student might be identified for Tier 3 intervention. This would also be a good time to arrange assessments that would help rule out other causes — in other words, to screen or test particular students for vision and hearing problems, for food allergies, or other possible medical explanations.

RTI Tier 3

Tier 3 interventions should be designed to intensify and individualize the programs, strategies, and procedures in order to supplement or enhance Tier 1 and Tier 2 supports — all with the goal of helping selected students become successful within their classroom. This third level of intervention might include significant adaptations, such as using assistive technology unique to the individual, or counselling supports, or speech and language programming, and so on.

When Tier 3 interventions do not lead to success for the student, the team should — for the first time — consider that the student could possibly have a learning disability.

Spotlight
For more information on RTI, visit
<www.rti4success.org>.

Guided by the results of a comprehensive evaluation, the teachers should establish initial goals, through an individual education plan (IEP), and ways of monitoring progress on an ongoing basis to direct the teaching process.

Role of the Resource Teacher in RTI

In RTI, the resource teacher can play one of three roles that correspond to the three tiers:

Tier 1: supporting inclusive instructional practice in classrooms

Tier 2: initiating an ecobehavioural assessment and subsequent programming for the classroom

Tier 3: arranging assessments of students who are struggling with the learning, and developing IEPs

This tiered approach creates a step-by-step process for teachers to follow as we support diverse learners. This process is not unique to the Three-Block Model nor to RTI or to UDL. It is the internationally recommended process for inclusive education. In subsequent chapters, we explore each of these tiers and describe in detail the corresponding role of the resource teacher. But to be clear:

1. The Three-Block Model emphasizes co-teaching in the general education classroom as the primary service delivery model.

2. The model emphasizes "push in" services over "pull-out" services at all three tiers.

3. The goal is always to achieve successful social and academic inclusion of each student.

Portage & Main Press, 2013, *Resource Teachers*, ISBN: 978-1-55379-501-8

Chapter 4

Tier 1 — Supporting Inclusive Instructional Practice

Key terms and concepts
- Collaborative skills and concepts
  - continuum of: consultation, collaboration, coaching (Three C's)
  - co-teaching
- Consultation skills
  - third point (neutral point in conflict resolution)
  - levels of abstraction

Essential understandings
- The role of the resource teacher has changed in an inclusive system to that of collaborator and teacher-leader.
- Previous practice assumed disability was located within students. Universal design recognizes that environments can be disabling.
- The role of educational assistants in an inclusive system is to facilitate the social and academic engagement of all students — not just students with disabilities.

Education systems did not initiate "special education." The term began to be used in hospitals and residential institutions in the 1950s when communities began to release patients from adult psychiatric institutions — a process of "deinstitutionalization." They recognized the need to also deinstitutionalize children, which initially led to the creation of special schools in the community. Like many group homes, these were segregated settings within the community but without facilitating actual interaction with community members. The model then progressed to special classrooms within regular schools, still with little or no contact between students with disabilities and typical peers. Gradually, integration evolved as a part-time process, often for non-academic times, and often with an educational assistant (EA) accompanying the children. Special education teachers had little or no contact with regular classroom teachers. The progression to inclusion began similarly, with EAs working with students in regular classrooms, and special education teachers (now called resource teachers, RTs) followed the

Portage & Main Press, 2013, *Resource Teachers*, ISBN: 978-1-55379-501-8

pull-out model, taking students out of the regular classrooms to work with them in a resource room.

At our current stage of inclusion, we treat resource teachers as just that — a resource. They work to assess learning difficulties, to adapt or modify curriculum for students with exceptional needs, and to deliver specialized programming, either within the class or in small-group pull-out settings. This model remains in place today. However, even as such inclusion has progressed, research has shown that students make their greatest progress when they spend the maximum amount of school time in the regular classroom with their age peers, but having "special education" supports provided in that classroom.

Disability and Disabling Environments

Are individuals disabled, or are environments disabling? Answers to this question are critical in shifting our thinking as educators. In any large group of adults, we find many who wear glasses or contact lenses. Without these supports, many would not be able to participate in traditional, text-based learning. In Canada, we provide the "prescription" for this type of disability, but what if you lived in a country where eyeglasses, contact lenses, and laser eye surgery were not available? Many individuals who are successful here in Canada would have to be bused to another school where they do less reading and use large print. Is the individual who needs glasses disabled, or is it the country that is disabling that individual by not providing the necessary supports? The disability is, indeed, in the individual whose retina is slightly convex or concave. In a country that does not provide glasses or eye care, that individual would have a visual impairment, and many would find life a struggle. But how helpful would it be to have their eyes tested, inform them and their parents that they have a visual impairment, and then suggest that they cannot possibly be successful in a regular classroom or job? Is the disability within them, or within the environment that does not meet or adjust to their needs?

In our history as educators, we have assumed that a disability is located in the individual. It is a profound shift in thinking and practice to consider, instead, that the environment we provide might be the disabling element. Because we don't have the right "prescription" for what many students need, we label them as impaired in some way. In the case of someone who needs glasses, we recognize that we can provide supports and that, when they are in place, the person will be able to participate fully both socially and academically. What prescription can we write for a student with attentional challenges or for the struggling reader? We do know many strategies we can use with these learners (chunking activities, allowing breaks for physical movement, listening to audio books, and so on), but we are often reluctant to do so in a systematic and non-judgmental way. By first considering the classroom environment and exploring what is not working before we test and label students, we are led to a whole new way of envisioning — and being — a resource teacher. Resource teachers must play a role in helping regular classroom teachers create inclusive environments that provide all learners full access to the learning

Portage & Main Press, 2013, *Resource Teachers*, ISBN: 978-1-55379-501-8

and life of the classroom. This puts RTs into the new role of "teacher-leader" or "professional developer."

Collaborative Practice

If we are to achieve social and academic inclusion for all students, and focus on supporting students so that they are successful in their classrooms, then the role of the resource teacher must become a collaborative role — working with other resource teachers, classroom teachers, administrators, clinicians, educational assistants, families, and students to coordinate services. This is fundamentally different from pulling kids out of the regular classroom to focus on remediation of skills in isolation from the regular classroom program and teacher. For Tier 2 or Tier 3 interventions, RTs must still conduct specialized assessments to guide interventions, but the goal will be to determine the strategies that can support the students within their classroom.

Collaborative teaching practices support both teachers and students and thereby improve learning and working environments (Little and Dieker 2009). The three main models of collaboration described in the literature are:

1. **consultation,** in which the RT advises the CT on strategies for supporting students with disabilities

2. **co-teaching,** in which the RT comes into the classroom for part of the day and supports instruction

3. **team teaching,** in which both teachers co-plan, co-teach, and co-assess (Austin 2001)

The team-teaching model involves the RT and the CT in a team approach to meeting the needs of all the students, not just the students with exceptional needs. It reduces territoriality and allows them to combine talents, knowledge, and energy. Such a team also reduces stigma for the students, normalizes differentiation, and creates a family and community atmosphere. The collaborative model is written into many Canadian educational policies. For instance, New Brunswick policy states:

> The model of Collaborative Consultation is one that is supported by the New Brunswick Department of Education, as it enhances the philosophy of inclusion and involves all stakeholders in planning, implementing and monitoring programs for students with exceptionalities. (New Brunswick Department of Education 2002, p. 9)

In this role, the resource teacher brings to the situation knowledge of issues in special education, just as the classroom teacher and others bring their knowledge of their areas of expertise. Together, they problem-solve and plan for the students. The resource teacher co-plans and co-teaches with the classroom teacher. Although this model is the ideal, resource teachers cannot be in any one classroom full-time, which means that it is imperative to develop the capacity of classroom teachers, because they have the primary responsibility for the education of diverse learners in their classroom.

Portage & Main Press, 2013, *Resource Teachers*, ISBN: 978-1-55379-501-8

In their book *Mentoring Matters*, Lipton and Wellman (2001) describe a continuum of support called the Three C's:

1. **Coaching:** The CT takes the lead and is supported by the RT. Wellman sees this as a positive indicator of the CT's self-efficacy.

2. **Collaborating:** A joint effort in which responsibility is shared. This is team-teaching.

3. **Consulting:** The RT is the expert, consulting with a new teacher or a CT who is feeling overwhelmed or in need of significant support.

I highly recommend this book to RTs who are trying to support CTs in using inclusive instructional practices. It is critical to know when to bring other people on board. Resource teachers should be prepared to take each stance of the Three C's:

1. **Consulting** when the colleague feels overwhelmed, or insecure, or needs to "see it"

2. **Collaborating** when the colleague is motivated, needs guided practice, or when two is better than one for the students' sake

3. **Coaching** when the colleague feels confident and is ready to manage independently

According to Lipton and Wellman, two aspects of such collegial interaction change in each stance of this continuum.

First, the exchange of information is different. In a **consulting** stance, the RTs provide the information, based on their expertise. In a **collaborative** exchange, both teachers brainstorm and research ideas. In a **coaching** stance, CTs provide the information, guided by inquiring and clarifying questions from the RT.

Second, the gap analysis is different. That is, in a **consulting** stance, the RT recognizes what the CT doesn't know, and provides the information. In a **collaborative** stance, the question becomes "What do we not know about this student, topic, or strategy that we need to know?" And in the **coaching** stance, the CT is the one to identify what they need to know or learn.

This continuum of support is very similar to any good teaching — a flexible range from direct instruction (**consulting**) to guided practice (**collaboration**) to independent application (**coaching**). Within any collegial relationship, RTs may need to assume any of the three roles at different times, depending on their relationship with the colleague, on the situation, and on the colleague's request. Being able to read a colleague or a situation and assess at which point to engage in the three C's continuum is important. For instance, entering as a consultant and giving unrequested advice to a senior colleague can be perceived as insulting, eliciting a "Who do you think you are?" response. In contrast, a teacher who is overwhelmed, anxious, and looking for a lifeline may feel unsupported by a coaching response of "You can do it."

Keep in mind that the goal is to develop capacity in the CT. The RT cannot be there full-time, so their goal is for the CTs to learn the strategies that can help them meet the needs of the diverse students in their class. The RT's job is to teach

Portage & Main Press, 2013, *Resource Teachers*, ISBN: 978-1-55379-501-8

the pedagogy of UDL. Some colleagues will gladly allow the RT to come in as the expert and take over, but then will not continue the UDL strategies when the RT leaves. This means that the RT must stick to the goal of empowering colleagues to take ownership, that is, the RT must take the role of collaborator or coach — in the same way that the CTs encourage their students to do. Chronological age or years of experience are not the deciding factors. A first-year teacher might be the expert on a new technique or strategy that a senior teacher does not know about — and vice versa.

When colleagues approach, the RT is wise to be cautious at first, to probe gently in order to determine what they really want. If a CT approaches and says, "I don't know what to do with Daniel. He just never gets anything done," what stance would you take? You might offer advice or suggestions (consulting), offer to come in and help (collaboration), or reassure them with a coaching stance, "Knowing you, I know you will find a way. You're always so good with the kids who struggle." Instead, asking a probing question such as "What do you think is breaking down for him?" or "Is there anything I can do to help?" leaves the dialogue open so you can determine what is being asked of you. A teacher's reply of "I have no idea. I'm completely lost with this kid" calls for a consulting or collaborating stance. In contrast, a reply like "Oh, he's just distractible — like half the kids I teach. I'm just going to have to break tasks down for him" suggests a coaching stance with a "Well, you certainly know how to support him" would be appreciated; that is, the teacher just needed to vent and be heard.

Co-Teaching

It's all about relationships. When working with their colleagues, teachers who are collaborating should:

TtD: pp. 139-142

1. approach each other as an equal
2. put oneself in the role of a supportive friend
3. share the workload — mark work, plan, intervene in behaviour
4. recognize each other's strengths, and defer to each other when needed
5. laugh and have fun
6. be willing to move through the continuum of the 3 C's, sometimes stepping in with expertise, sometimes as a partner, sometimes stepping back and letting the CT run the show

RTs have two goals in this role:

1. Support *all* students in the class socially and academically. As long as RTs think it's their job to focus on the students *with* disabilities, CTs will think their own job is to focus on the students *without* disabilities. RTs must share the teaching of all kids, if they want the CTs to take ownership of all students.

2. Develop your colleague's capacity to meet the needs of diverse learners, that is, pursue the principles of universal design for learning.

Many RTs hesitate to co-teach for two reasons. *First*, they are concerned about philosophical differences, assuming that two teachers must have similar philosophies or styles if they are to agree on how to support Johnny. But teachers do not have to fully share strategies or philosophies in order to co-teach — just as we expect students, working in cooperative groups, to "work it out" although they don't agree on the best method. In fact, co-teaching provides an opportunity to peer-coach, to recognize that although we two are not currently in synch, our goal is to get to that place, over time. *Second*, some RTs worry about being seen as glorified EAs, floating around the classroom to support exceptional students while the teacher teaches. Again, such a concern harks back to the original belief that RTs intervene only by taking students out of the classroom for direct instruction. Once we all acknowledge that what's best for these students is staying in the class with their peers, we can view our role as a teacher of all the students. We can also consider the strategy of "one teaching, one supporting" as an excellent opportunity to conduct an ecobehavioural assessment, by observing the learning environment and the students and by coaching our colleagues.

Using a third point to address difficult situations

A third point allows teachers to focus on a neutral object or idea that is the real issue when resolving conflicts. The third point depersonalizes the situation so that the teachers can problem solve. As an example: You assign a math problem, and one student reacts, saying, "This is stupid. I'm not doing this." Rather than engage in a power struggle — "You can do this now or at recess" — which is not really a choice, use the problem or task as a third point and say, "Okay. Tell me what it is about this that doesn't work for you?" Such an approach allows the student to blame the task — it's not that either of you is stupid; it's the task, and the task has no ego, so no hurt feelings. The student replies, "It's dumb. How are we supposed to ….", indicating the part of the task that's not clear. Such an indirect tactic in response to a direct challenge can defuse a potentially explosive issue without putting relationships at risk.

Similarly, suppose a colleague approaches and says, "I'm fed up with Johnny. He gets nothing done unless I'm right beside him, but I have 30 other students to consider." Find a third point to address how the teacher might support Johnny — and other students like him — who might be struggling with long, oral, multi-step directions for their tasks. By saying, "Let's look at some of Johnny's work and see where he is breaking down," you place the teacher's focus on the work samples, not on Johnny, and not on the teacher's instructional style. When looking at the work, try comments such as "It appears that Johnny does okay when the task has only one step. Do you think his difficulty occurs when the task has several steps?" Such a strategy could allow you and the teacher to brainstorm:

"Can the steps be chunked?"

Portage & Main Press, 2013, *Resource Teachers*, ISBN: 978-1-55379-501-8

"Should we put instructions on the board?"

"Should students work as partners to support Johnny and any others who are struggling?"

Shifting levels of abstraction

People do get stuck sometimes, and are unable to grow and change because of the level of their focus. When taking a "big picture" view, they may become overwhelmed. When narrowing their focus, they see only the details, and become lost in them. In both cases, RTs can help shift the level of abstraction in such a way that resolution seems possible. By paraphrasing what a teacher says, the RT can shift levels. For example, if you want to shift the teacher's view of the issue up a level or two, you could say something like, "I see you want to help Johnny and your other students become more independent learners." This viewpoint shifts the issue from dealing with seemingly oppositional, or challenging, behaviour to setting a goal for Johnny that you can be dealt with by devising strategies for helping get him there. If, on the other hand, the teacher is generalizing a problem and making it seem large and overwhelming, you can shift down by saying, "You've noticed that Johnny has difficulty following multi-step directions." Again, this shift down can lead the two of you into a conversation about strategies.

Working with Educational Assistants

In an inclusive school, teachers work with all children and so do educational assistants (EAs), who are considered paraprofessionals. Research has shown that the practice of assigning EAs one-on-one to students with special needs is highly detrimental to those students' social and academic inclusion (Giangreco 2010). The primary role of an educational assistant is to promote the engagement and inclusion of all students, helping them remain engaged in classroom activities, interacting respectfully with their peers, and feeling valued. Sometimes, it is difficult to distinguish between when it's appropriate to provide paraprofessional support to a student and when doing so might cause problems. When in doubt, members of the teaching team should ask themselves, "Would this situation be acceptable if the student did not have a disability?" (Giangreco and Doyle 2002).

Consider the following situations:

- A paraprofessional provides the student's primary literacy instruction.
- The student is removed from class activities at the discretion of the paraprofessional rather than the teacher.
- The student spends 80 percent or more of his or her time with a paraprofessional.

Portage & Main Press, 2013, *Resource Teachers*, ISBN: 978-1-55379-501-8

- The student spends the majority of his or her social time (lunch, recess) with a paraprofessional rather than with classmates.
- The paraprofessional, rather than the teacher or special educator, makes the majority of day-to-day curricular and instructional decisions affecting the student.

Such situations highlight a double standard as most educators would consider them unacceptable for students *without* disabilities, yet they occur all too frequently for students *with* disabilities.

Educational assistants play a valuable role in a learning community. They help to maintain the cohesion of the community by facilitating all students' engagement in the learning. They can assist the classroom teachers with the implementation of IEPs for students with exceptional needs, but only when the goals are aimed at their social and academic inclusion in the class. Having EAs work with such students at the back of the room is not inclusive, nor is asking EAs to take students out of the classroom.

We must remember that EAs are not teachers and, therefore, they should not be asked to design programs or to assess the exceptional students. The classroom teacher holds primary responsibility for designing the instruction with the help of the resource teacher. However, as members of the educational team, EAs can support the health and safety of the classroom community, provide unique knowledge of individual students, and facilitate the development of an inclusive community.

If we extend our example of the medical field, having our neediest learners taught by our least trained personnel is like handing the Emergency Room or the Intensive Care Unit to the orderlies. As a profession, we must recognize the inappropriateness of this model, and work to correct it, rather than demanding more and more EAs for every child who is struggling. As we develop our ability to meet the needs of diverse learners through universal design for learning, we must restructure the role of the EA to what it was originally intended to be — an assistant, not the primary provider.

Portage & Main Press, 2013, *Resource Teachers*, ISBN: 978-1-55379-501-8

Chapter 5
Ecobehavioural Assessment in Tier 1 and Tier 2

Key terms and concepts
- universal design for learning (UDL)
- Three-Block Model of UDL
- mental models and assessment frameworks
- multiple intelligences
- neurodevelopmental constructs
- ecobehavioural assessment

Essential understandings
- UDL is a conceptual framework for planning and instruction that provide accessibility for all learners to the social and academic life of the classroom.
- The Three-Block Model of UDL synthesizes the research on effective practices for inclusive education to provide teachers with practical ways of applying them in K to 12 classrooms.
- Ecobehavioural assessment involves observing the environment in which students learn, identifying ecological factors and barriers to inclusion, and adapting the environment, rather than remediating the child.
- Neurodevelopment means the development of brain functions, in this case, functions related to learning such as attention and memory.
- Neurodevelopmental constructs can be divided into subcategories such as working memory, short-term memory, and long-term memory.

Globally, across decades and populations, research has demonstrated that inclusive education greatly benefits both students with disabilities and those without (Curcic 2009; Kalambouka, Farrell, Dyson, and Kaplan 2007). In recent years, with this knowledge, we have shifted from "Is it possible?" and "Does it work?" or "Why should we do it?" to the how-to. Extensive research has documented hundreds of strategies for supporting inclusive education (McLeskey, Rosenberg, and Westling 2010). However, from a classroom teacher's standpoint, it is unclear how to apply all of these strategies in a holistic, practical manner that works in all grades (K–12) and in a variety of settings (rural, urban, inner city, multi-grade) — which is the goal of UDL (King-Sears 2009).

Portage & Main Press, 2013, *Resource Teachers*, ISBN: 978-1-55379-501-8

Universal Design for Learning

The terms *universal design* and *universal design for learning* are often confused. Universal design comes from the field of architecture (Mace, Story, and Mueller 1998). When architects were exploring the issues of physical accessibility to buildings with front stairs, they acknowledged that reconstructing a building to add ramps, widen doorways, lower countertops, and so on is expensive and labour-intensive. Besides, it never truly resulted in equal access because the ramps were usually placed at the side or the back of the building, the washrooms were separate, and only one or two rooms or counters were actually accessible. Architects design the entrances of buildings to provide a specific experience to the entrant. Whether the lobby is designed to provide a feeling of glamour or expansiveness, efficiency or warmth, one is meant to have a particular emotional experience, and to learn something about the purpose of the building when one enters.

When people in wheelchairs have to enter from a side entrance or back door, as can happen with retrofitting, they are denied the intended experience. Using separate washrooms or other facilities also segregated people with disabilities. Sound familiar? We are currently retrofitting our educational systems. We design our units and lessons, then decide what activities Johnny will do. We call it adapting or modifying our curriculum, but in the language of architecture, it is retrofitting. As in architecture, the retrofitting in education has become expensive because it takes time and resources to build a ramp for every "special" child, especially as the numbers grow. When you enter a building through a side door, you don't have the same experience as others. In education, the student with special needs enters "through a side door" by being pulled out of a classroom to a resource room, or by working with an educational assistant at the back of the classroom, or by having a workbook or photocopied sheets of tasks from earlier grades. These students do not have the same learning experience as the students who "entered through the front door" because they are not participating as part of the class.

The term *universal design* was coined by Ronald Mace (1998), an architect, who faced the question "How do you design in such a way as to be accessible for the most participants possible, without lowering standards?" As architects began to respond to the challenge in their designs, they discovered that many people actually benefit from the additional options. In the Vancouver airport, for example, people can enter the building using an elevator or an escalator, a ramp or stairs. All points of entry converge in the same place. Although the ramp was originally meant for people with disabilities to use, it now also serves parents with strollers, travellers with wheeled cases, and many others. Another excellent example is that of ramped curbs. Initially designed to allow people in wheelchairs independence when travelling around the city, many unintended populations benefited, and the experience of those capable of stepping up onto the curb was not diminished.

This metaphor of accessibility was brought forward into education as "universal design for learning," but there the similarity ends. Initially, educators tried to adopt the criteria of universal design in architecture as evident in the educational

Portage & Main Press, 2013, *Resource Teachers*, ISBN: 978-1-55379-501-8

literature referencing flexible use, simplicity of use, and similar phrases. However, this transference was artificial, and educators soon realized that what creates accessibility to tools and to physical spaces differs from accessibility to learning and to social interactions. More recent development of the theory and practice of UDL recognizes a wide range of pedagogies that facilitate accessibility for diverse learners, including both social and emotional practices and instructional practices (Burgstahler and Chang 2009). Almost every discussion of UDL is peppered with references to "access," but despite having access to a building or access to a classroom, one can still not be really included. We must take "access" one step further — to "involvement." Meaningful involvement in a learning community means that *all* students are active participants in the learning, and that they have meaningful interactions with their peers. We must also wrestle with the term "meaningful." For instance, it is challenging to determine

> Now, here is the deeper level of thinking when it comes to UDL — "access" is not enough!

how a student with significant disabilities can be meaningfully involved in a secondary school class (I address that question in chapter 13). However, we face this challenge with more students than those with a significant disability. Attributes of gender, race, sexual orientation, language proficiency, and social skills all contribute to the challenge.

How does the student who is LGBTQ participate meaningfully in a health class when the curriculum focuses dominantly on heterosexual concepts of "how babies are conceived?" Think about a First Nations student when the theme for a unit is on "first contact." Female students, participating in a study unit on the world wars, often encounter texts and resources in which the only portrayal of women's roles is as nurses. Such mismatches between students' personal experiences and the curricula can be barriers to some students' meaningful participation and, hence, their engagement in the content. Education is a complex endeavour in which multiple forces must work together. Figure 5.1 represents how the social and cognitive aspects of inclusive education work together in powerful ways.

In order to achieve social inclusion, students must have a sense of their self-worth, of belonging and of being involved in meaningful interactions with their peers. Being helped by a peer to do a task is not a social interaction based on equity and friendship — which should be a goal for all students. To achieve that level of interaction, we must ensure that all students have socially valued roles, and we must emphasize continuously the need to respect diverse others. For a student to be academically included, they must be challenged cognitively, participate meaningfully in the academic tasks of the class, and have opportunities to encounter other perspectives and ideas through peer interactions, all of which becomes part of critical thinking. Going one step further, the two constructs also indirectly affect one another. For example, if people have no sense of self-worth, how can they persevere through a cognitively challenging task? In an academic setting, students develop self-worth through successful completion of challenging tasks. Therefore, when a teacher gives students a task they cannot be successful

Portage & Main Press, 2013, *Resource Teachers*, ISBN: 978-1-55379-501-8

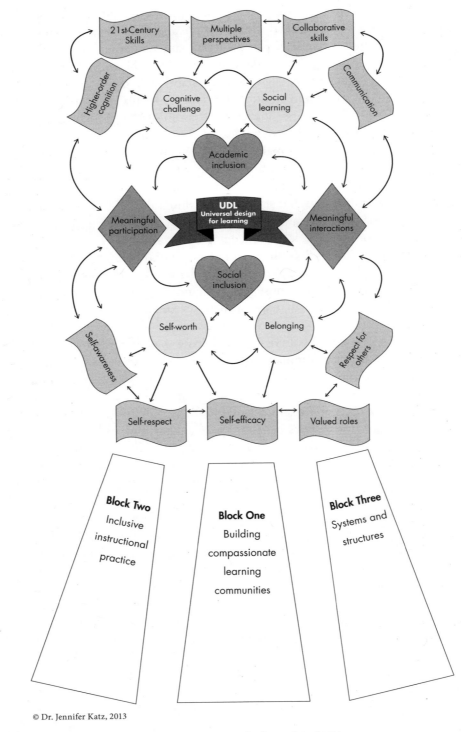

© Dr. Jennifer Katz, 2013

Figure 5.1 Theoretical framework of the Three-Block Model of UDL

in or, alternatively, that is too easy for them, they cannot experience a sense of success, and develop self-worth that will lead to engagement and perseverance in learning. We have the result — many students who disengage from schooling, including many of our gifted learners.

UDL has been shown to support access, participation, and progress for all learners (Jimenez, Graf, and Rose 2007; King-Sears 2009; Kortering, McLannon, and Braziel 2008; Meo 2012; Rose and Meyer 2002). However, few have provided a comprehensive framework to put the pieces together in a practical, research-grounded, efficient manner for K to 12. There are three key components to inclusive education: a) building safe learning communities, b) inclusive instructional practice, and c) systemic supports. These are also the essence of my Three-Block Model of UDL. Several provinces have mandated UDL as a means of creating inclusive classrooms. The following excerpt on Manitoba policy (*Appropriate Educational Programming*) is incorporated in Bill 13 (Manitoba Education, Citizenship and Youth 2006):

> When applied to the field of education, the concept of universal design means that school communities, including teachers, develop plans for the full diversity of their student population. In education, universally designed schools, classrooms, curricula and materials provide all students with access to the resources they require, regardless of their diverse learning needs.

It is clear that inclusion and universal design are not only our jobs as educators, they are actually the law.

As discussed, the role of the resource teacher is to support classroom teachers in implementing UDL in their classrooms, and to help students become successful in their classrooms. To the greatest extent possible, all students should be participating alongside their peers, and supports should be delivered to the whole class rather than singling out, and thereby stigmatizing, individual students. It is necessary, therefore, that all RTs be familiar with planning, instruction, and assessment in a UDL classroom.

Spotlight

For more information, visit: <www.udlcenter.org> and <www.inclusiveeducation.ca>; <www.cast.org> and <www.threeblockmodel.com>.

Mental Models: Assessment Frameworks

It is important that when we conduct an assessment of any kind, we use a framework for assessing student achievement. For instance, when assessing *reading comprehension*, we look for the student's ability to recall the main events, infer meanings, make connections, create mental images, and so on. When we look at the bigger picture of a student's *learning*, we need a framework through which we can observe their strengths and relative challenges. In my work as an RT, I used two frameworks to develop student learning profiles — multiple intelligences (MI) and neurodevelopmental constructs.

Portage & Main Press, 2013, *Resource Teachers*, ISBN: 978-1-55379-501-8

Multiple Intelligences

The theory of multiple intelligences (MI) recognizes that the brain processes information in many different ways. We know, for instance, that visual information travels from the eye along the optic nerve to the visual cortex, and then to the frontal lobe for recognition, one of the physical pathways in the brain. In contrast, sound travels from the auditory canal to the auditory cortex, and then on to various parts of the brain, depending on whether the sound comes from music, from words, or from the environment. We all know that students learn in many different ways, and that all of us have relative strengths and challenges within these modalities. Some of us are more verbal, others more visual. Descriptions of the nine intelligences provide a mental model for us when assessing a student's learning profile (see Figure 5.2, page 41). Most educators are familiar with MI, and the concept provides a helpful common language for discussing learning profiles and differentiating learning programs.

Neurodevelopmental Constructs

The term *neurodevelopment* encompasses the physical process of anatomical interconnections in the brain, the basis for the development of brain functions. In education, this process encompasses the constructs related to learning — attention, memory, language processing, and so on. Neuro-developmental constructs, like memory, can be grouped into subcategories such as working memory, short-term memory, and long-term memory. Students have relative strengths and challenges in neurodevelopmental constructs, but a significant challenge faced by any student can develop into a learning disability. The brain processes that underlie learning have eight neurodevelopmental constructs (see pp. 43–47).

Affinities

Children's interests and affinities; that is, their natural inclinations, also affect learning. Affinities influence a person's motivation and, thus, their background knowledge and vocabulary, as well as their memory and attention.

Environmental factors

Children live in different family structures, cultures, and communities, which means they differ in experiences, background knowledge, vocabulary, and other attributes. Other environmental factors that influence development are nutrition, sleep, and attitudes.

Spotlight

To familiarize yourself with the neurodevelopmental framework, visit <www.allkindsofminds.org>. The book *Educational Care* (Levine 2002) has a chapter on each of the neurodevelopmental constructs with suggestions for supports. All people have relative learning strengths and challenges that can be illustrated on a bar graph (see "Multiple Intelligences Surveys" in Appendix of *Teaching to Diversity*).

Portage & Main Press, 2013, *Resource Teachers*, ISBN: 978-1-55379-501-8

Intelligence	Definition	Abilities	Careers
VERBAL–LINGUISTIC	Has the capacity to develop verbal skills and sensitivity to the sounds, meanings, and rhythms of words. These learners do well in language-based activities.	Listening, reading, speaking, writing	Journalist, lawyer, translator, author, teacher
LOGICAL–MATHEMATICAL	Has the ability to think conceptually and abstractly and the capacity to discern logical or numerical patterns. These learners do well with numbers and problem solving.	Mental calculation, pattern recognition, problem solving, research and experimentation	Researcher, scientist, accountant, mathematician, economist
MUSICAL–RHYTHMIC	Has the ability to produce and appreciate rhythm, pitch and timbre. These learners learn best when things are presented in a chant, have a rhythm or pattern, and when "teacher talk" is not monotone.	Composing, making connections between emotions and sounds or tone; singing; playing an instrument	Sound engineer, sound effects producer, musician, composer, disc jockey
VISUAL–SPATIAL	Has the ability to visualize in detail, the capacity to think in images and pictures, accurately and abstractly. This ability is more than just artistic; it is the ability to visualize concepts such as a molecule or a fraction.	Design, spatial awareness, constructing, artistic representation	Architect, engineer, designer (graphic, interior), inventor, artist, sculptor, orienteer, guide
BODILY–KINESTHETIC	Has the ability to control one's bodily movements and to handle objects skillfully. These learners excel in hands-on tasks such as building models and conducting experiments.	Construction, athletics, crafts (e.g., art, sewing, woodworking), acting, dance	Builder, craftsman, craftswoman, surgeon, nurse, worker in the trades, seamstress, actor, athlete, dancer
INTERPERSONAL	Has the capacity to detect and respond appropriately to the moods, motivations, and desires of others. These learners work well in groups, and are often leaders.	Collaboration, empathy, counselling, relationship building, politics, leadership	Management role, politician, counsellor, sales and marketing representative, person involved in business or international relations

Figure 5.2 Synopsis of the multiple intelligences (MI)

Portage & Main Press, 2013, *Resource Teachers*, ISBN: 978-1-55379-501-8

INTRAPERSONAL	Has the capacity to be self-aware and in tune with inner feelings, values, beliefs, and thinking processes. These learners have strength in metacognition; they know how they learn, and what challenges them.	Reflection, meta-cognition, emotional intelligence	Poet, journalist, lyricist, theorist
NATURALIST	Has the ability to recognize and categorize plants, animals and other objects in nature. These learners learn best through inquiry and discovery; they excel in categorization such as scientific classification.	Categorizing, recognizing patterns, seeing connection among all living things, applying scientific theory to experiences	Botanist, biologist, landscape architect, farmer, zoologist, hiking guide
EXISTENTIAL	Has sensitivity and the capacity to tackle deep questions about human existence: the meaning of life; Why do we die? How did we get here? In order to be engaged, these learners need to know why what they are learning is important, and how it can impact on a larger scale.	Gestalt thinking, global thinking, abstraction, making inferences, spiritual awareness	Theologian, scientist, philosopher, spiritual leader

Figure 5.2 cont'd

Portage & Main Press, 2013, *Resource Teachers*, ISBN: 978-1-55379-501-8

Construct	Description	Red Flags that help identify a student challenged by this construct:	Behaviours that help identify this construct as a student's strength:
1. ATTENTION	This construct is more than just "paying attention." It includes the ability to concentrate, to focus on one thing at a time, to finish the tasks one begins, and to control what one says and does. a. mental energy — initiating and maintaining the flow of energy needed for cognitive work output; sustaining attention b. processing controls — regulating the use of incoming information; screening out distractions c. production controls — regulating academic and behavioural output; controlling impulsivity.	• incomplete work • organizational challenges • distractibility • fatigue • movement • impulsivity • work that starts off well, but doesn't finish, or error rate increases, or work is rushed	• ability to sustain attention for long periods of time when interested • ability to screen out background noise such as people walking by, movements of peers, chatter, and so on • tendency to think before responding, and planning a response.
2. SOCIAL COGNITION	The most often overlooked component of learning is the ability to succeed in social relationships with peers, parents, and teachers. Students (and adults) may be strong in other construct areas, and yet have academic difficulties because of an inability to make friends, work in groups, or cope effectively with peer pressure. a. verbal pragmatics — using and understanding language within social contexts. Knows that one speaks differently to their friends than to adults, and that one speaks differently in different places, for instance, at home, in church/temple/ mosque/synagogue b. social behaviours — acting in a way that fosters optimal relationships with others c. political acumen — nurturing positive relationships with important people, particularly adults; knowing how to work the system	• often alone • inappropriate with peers • speaks to everyone as though they are the same level of intimacy • "I was just joking!" — cannot recognize when others might not find him or his actions funny • unable to read emotions, tone of voice • interprets literature incorrectly in terms of emotions, relationships • makes inaccurate attempts at being "cool"	• changes "voice," depending on audience and situation • looked to as a leader by peers • known by many adults in the school, seen as a role model

Figure 5.3 Overview of Eight Neurodevelopmental Constructs

Portage & Main Press, 2013, *Resource Teachers*, ISBN: 978-1-55379-501-8

Construct	Description	Red Flags that help identify a student challenged by this construct:	Behaviours that help identify this construct as a student's strength:
3. HIGHER-ORDER COGNITION	This construct describes the ability to understand, and implement, the steps necessary to solve problems, attack new areas of learning, make sense of new concepts, and think creatively. a. concept formation/transformation — integrating a series of features that often go together to form a class of ideas or objects b. critical thinking — evaluate products, ideas, and opinions c. creativity — thinking independently and producing self-generated thoughts or other products d. problem solving — applying a systematic stepwise approach to complex questions or challenges e. rule use — learning, developing, and applying rules and principles f. logical thinking, reasoning — coming up with sensible, thoughtful answers to complex issues g. mental representation — portraying new ideas in one's mind so they are most meaningful and lasting	• memorizes, but cannot generalize learning • has difficulty with connections • decodes, but doesn't comprehend • cannot "read between the lines," make inferences • poor problem solving skills	• ability to synthesize, analyze • thinks "outside the box," creative • makes unusual and deep connections • sees "the big picture" • metacognitive

4. LANGUAGE	Being able to articulate and understand language is central to the ability to do well as students and learners. Developing language functions involves elaborate interactions between variousparts of the brwain because it involves so many separate abilities: pronouncing words, awareness of different sounds, comprwehending written symbols, understanding syntax, and telling stories.	• receptive
		  o requires repetition of instructions, ideas
		  o looks puzzled, confused
		  o asks questions that were just answered
		  o begins tasks with last step given in instructions
		  o needs to read it rather than hear it
			• receptive
			  o able to process multi-step directions
			  o interprets teacher talk to other students ("she said...", or "she means...")
			  o asks appropriate clarifying questions

Figure 5.3 cont'd

Portage & Main Press, 2013, *Resource Teachers*, ISBN: 978-1-55379-501-8

Construct	Description	Red Flags that help identify a student challenged by this construct:	Behaviours that help identify this construct as a student's strength:

4. LANGUAGE (cont'd)	a. receptive language— processing and understanding incoming oral and written information
	b. expressive language — communicating and producing ideas orally and in writing
		• expressive
		  ○ frequent "tip of tongue" search for words
		  ○ talks a lot; describes in great detail what could be said in one word
		  ○ uses vague language "It's that thing, y' know…"
		  ○ talks very little; uses gesture or drawing to explain ideas or just withdraws
			• expressive
			  ○ is concise, articulate, eloquent (for their age)
			  ○ has advanced vocabulary
			  ○ looked to by others for explanation

5. NEUROMOTOR FUNCTIONS	Whether students are trying to write their first words, catch a football, or punch away at a computer keyboard, their brains' ability to coordinate their motor or muscle functions are key to many areas of learning.
	a. gross motor function — using large muscles in a coordinated, effective manner
	b. fine motor function — demonstrating effective manual dexterity
	c. graphomotor function — manoeuvring a utensil to produce handwriting
	**Many people confuse the latter two, but they are not the same neurologically. To draw artistically, information moves from the frontal lobe, to the visual cortex, to the motor cortex, and out the hand. To write, information comes from the language centres, to the motor cortex, and out the hand. It is, therefore, possible to have good fine-motor ability, but poor graphomotor ability, and vice versa. The fact that a student can draw does not mean they can write.
		• gross motor
		  ○ poor coordination
		  ○ avoids sports, recess, leisure activities
		  ○ sits in unusual positions
		• fine motor
		  ○ unusual pencil grasp
		  ○ poor printing and drawing skills
		  ○ difficulty with zippers, buttons, and such
		• graphomotor
		  ○ printing is illegible, but student can draw reasonably
		  ○ student's hand tires quickly
		  ○ student's work shows reversals in letter and word sequences
			• gross motor
			  ○ enjoys sports and being active
			  ○ learns well by doing, or by constructing; hands-on
			• fine motor
			  ○ neat printing
			  ○ skill with small movements — drawing, sewing, fixing things, playing an instrument
			• graphomotor
			  ○ able to sustain writing for a long period of time
			  ○ little or no difference between keyboarding and handwriting in level of production

Figure 5.3 cont'd

Portage & Main Press, 2013, *Resource Teachers*, ISBN: 978-1-55379-501-8

Construct	Description	Red Flags that help identify a student challenged by this construct:	Behaviours that help identify this construct as a student's strength:
6. TEMPORAL-SEQUENTIAL ORDERING	A key component of student learning is the ability to understand time and sequence — whether it's the ability to recite the alphabet, to skip-count, or to follow multi-step directions. a. sequential awareness and perception — being alert to the presence of and to identify an incoming sequence b. sequential memory — retaining the order of steps, events, or other sequences c. sequential output — creating products in which the content is arranged in the optimal order d. time management — using time efficiently e. higher sequential thinking — using serial order to enhance concept development and problem solving	• approaches tasks in an inappropriate or out-of-order sequence • cannot follow multi-step directions • exhibits poor time management • cannot tell, or retell, stories in a logical sequence • has difficulty with sequential mathematics such as counting and concepts of "more" and "less" • may spell words with correct letters, but out of order	• monitors time, prompts others ("Hey, guys, we only have 10 minutes left.") • can follow multi-step directions; reminds others • excels in mathematics, especially all Numbers strands
7. SPATIAL AWARENESS	Closely related to the functions of time and sequence is the ability to distinguish between a circle and a square, for example, or to use images to remember related information. On a more complex level, a musician's ability to "see" a piano keyboard and an architect's to "imagine" the shape of a particular room exemplify skill in spatial ordering. a. spatial awareness and perception — being alert to the presence of and identifying an incoming configuration b. spatial memory — storing and recalling shapes, symbols, and images c. spatial output — creating products that have spatial characteristics d. higher spatial thinking — reasoning and conceptualizing without language by using mental imagery	• has a poor sense of direction • has difficulty distinguishing shapes, visual details • often bumps into things • has difficulty with keyboarding • has difficulty copying from the board • has difficulty imagining a different visual perspective such as what something would look like from above, or from below, or from the other side	• uses descriptive language and detail • has a good sense of direction • had good hand-eye coordination • excels in geometry • is perceptive visually; appreciates art • uses visual imagery to remember • can take multiple visual perspectives and rotate images mentally

Figure 5.3 cont'd

Portage & Main Press, 2013, *Resource Teachers*, ISBN: 978-1-55379-501-8

Construct	Description	Red Flags that help identify a student challenged by this construct:	Behaviours that help identify this construct as a student's strength:
8. MEMORY	In the moment, a person may be able to understand, organize, and interpret the most complex information but if they cannot store and later recall that information, their performance often suffers dramatically. a. short-term memory — briefly registering new information that is used, stored, or forgotten b. active working memory — mentally suspending information while using or manipulating it c. long-term memory — permanently stored information, including knowledge, skills, and experiences, with ability to retrieve when wanted or needed	• requires frequent repetition of instructions • has organizational challenges • has difficulty with longer pieces, does well when information is chunked • often forgets "what I wanted to say" • shrugs when asked specific questions • "loses" skills that they had previously mastered	• can hold multi-step directions in memory, follow them one at a time • can problem solve • shows little difference between handwriting and keyboarding. Keyboarding requires less memory because it involves recognition rather than recall of letter formation; so if memory is a strength, writing is just as easy as keyboarding. • easily recalls rote facts (multiplication tables, spelling, sight words)

Figure 5.3 cont'd

Portage & Main Press, 2013, *Resource Teachers*, ISBN: 978-1-55379-501-8

Ecobehavioural Assessment in a UDL Context

Resource teachers should consider ecobehavioural assessment as a starting point in the Tier 2 intervention process. Some are quick to locate disability within the individual, but by universal design principles, first consider that some aspects of the environment may be disabling the individual. Before assessing individual students, we should first assess the interaction between the individual and their environment. Not every environment, teaching style, or activity is ideal for every student. When a student demonstrates a behavioural or learning issue, the first step should be to explore the match between the student's learning profile and the learning environment. Such a step does not suggest that the teacher is "a bad teacher" or that the student is "a bad kid " — rather, that the RT should consider whether there is a mismatch. For instance, if a student learns best visually but the teacher tends to give instructions orally, that's a mismatch, and may lead to learning or behaviour challenges. The reverse situation of a teacher who tends to write instructions on the board and a student who learns best by listening or observing is equally a mismatch.

Ecobehavioural assessment means just this: Observe the ecology of the classroom environment and its connection to the behaviour. For what length of time are students expected to listen? What grouping structures does the teacher commonly use? What types of tasks are prevalent? If you notice that the student pays attention when visuals are offered or when in small-group activities, but tends to be off-task when long instructions are given or when he is working independently, you can suggest adjusting practices to better suit his learning style — and perhaps that of many others by that adjustment.

A detailed ecobehavioural assessment is not always needed. However, noting your observations of such students — when you see them display desired behaviours and academic success, when you see they are struggling — helps guide the intervention plan. In UDL, we look first for what could be done within the classroom that would benefit all students, for example, chunking instructions, creating visual schedules, or having students partner and share their understanding of instructions might help that one student and many of his classmates as well. Instead of gluing a visual schedule to a student's desk, which singles them out, why not place it on the board? Many students will benefit from seeing what they need to get done, and what is coming next. One student who needs a break for physical movement can highlight the need that all their peers have, but try hard to control. Why not have the whole class take a stretch break, do a yoga pose or two by their desks, and then return to work? As a resource teacher, ask yourself:

What strategies could we use to support this student being successful in the classroom?

Could we do that for all the students, rather than singling this student out?

Portage & Main Press, 2013, *Resource Teachers*, ISBN: 978-1-55379-501-8

Try This: Mrs. Doe and son Jim

Mrs. Doe, Jim Doe's mother, telephones you, the resource teacher, to ask for help with her son. She is concerned that Jim is having difficulty completing schoolwork and organizing his materials, and he has begun avoiding homework assignments. She tells you that Jim denies that he has homework, but then Jim's classroom teacher calls her to say that he is not paying attention in class, rushes through his work, and does not complete his homework. When she asks Jim why he didn't tell her, he lowers his head and shuts down, refusing to talk. When asked about Jim's strengths and interests, she brightens up, saying that he has great verbal skills and creative thinking. He sings in a boy's choir, composes his own music, and wants to learn to meditate. She describes him as a "good kid" and a "bright boy" and she cannot understand why he lies about his homework.

You check with Jim's classroom teacher, who confirms what Mrs. Doe said: Jim is a bright kid and gets along well with everyone, but he is unfocused and seems not to care about his schoolwork. He just rushes through to get it done, and never brings back any homework.

What are your first thoughts about what might be happening for Jim?

We have to see Jim within his classroom in order to know what is not working for him. There are two aspects to our observations:

1. General observations

   a. What is the learning environment in which Jim is immersed?

   b. How is the classroom set up physically? Where is Jim seated?

   c. What kinds of tasks and grouping structures are used?

   d. How does the day flow (e.g., lots of short tasks with transitions; long tasks where sustained attention is required)?

2. Student-specific observations (evidence of strengths and weaknesses):

   a. When does he pay attention? When doesn't he?

   b. Are there some types of work where he takes his time and works carefully?

   c. What happens at the end of the day? Does he take his books home? Does he write down his homework?

   d. What kinds of tasks is Jim required to do over the course of the day?

   e. Are there times in the day when he is more focused than other times?

   f. Knowing that he likes music and spirituality (an existential thinker), what opportunities are there for him to learn through his strengths?

It is best to conduct several observations, at different times of the day and across different subjects, in order to get an overview of how Jim functions in class.

Analysis of Try This Scenario

If you said that he has "attentional issues," you would not be alone. But there are many possible reasons why Jim is struggling. Perhaps he has a memory deficit and knows that if he says "I forgot," no one will believe him. Perhaps he has graphomotor challenges, but knows that because he can share his ideas orally, no one will believe that he cannot write them down. There are many, many possibilities here. Before you talk to Jim, you can nevertheless suspect from what you've been told that Jim has some strengths (musical-rhythmic, oral verbal-linguistic, existential, social cognition, higher-order cognition), and he faces some challenges (attention? memory? graphomotor?). We cannot know for sure, however, until we conduct further assessment. So where do we start?

Try This: Observing Jim Doe

Imagine you go into Jim's classroom, and make the following observations.

SETTING EVENTS	Time of Day: 9:00 Activity: Desks, writing Grouping: Whole class, Individual		
Time	**Antecedent**	**Behaviour**	**Consequence**
9:00	Teacher giving instructions	Attentive	None
9:10	ditto	Fidgeting, looking in desk	None
9:20	Transition – getting materials out	Looking at peers, confused	Teacher prompts
9:25	Teacher reviews criteria, asks students to get started	Attentive	None
9:30	Writing	Attentive	None
9:35	At desk, other students working	Looking around, puts head on desk	Teacher prompts to "keep going"
9:40	Writing	Shaking hand out, writing	None
9:45	At desk, other students working	Hands in work, returns to desk	Teacher calls Jim up; asks him to add more detail
9:50	Returns to desk	Talking to peer, drawing	Teacher reminds Jim he needs to write not just draw
9:55	ditto	Closes book; head down on desk	Teacher informs Jim he will need to stay in at recess to complete

Figure 5.4 Observation #1

Portage & Main Press, 2013, Resource Teachers, ISBN: 978-1-55379-501-8

SETTING EVENTS	Time of Day: 10:30 Activity: Math Grouping: Whole class, Individual		
Time	**Antecedent**	**Behaviour**	**Consequence**
10:30	At desks, teacher modelling math procedure on board. Students have Cuisinaire rods on desk	Attentive	None
10:35	Students working on math sheet, with counters to assist	Using counters, attempting task	None
10:37	ditto	Head on desk	Teacher asks "How are you doing?"
10:38	ditto	Jim says "I'm tired"	Teacher prompts to speak French, then assists with next question
10:40	ditto	On task	None
10:45	ditto	Talking to neighbour	Teacher prompts to "stay focused"
10:50	ditto	Asks to go to washroom	Leaves room
Remainder of period	ditto	Returns in 15 minutes, puts sheet away	Page is given as homework

Figure 5.5 Observation #2

SETTING EVENTS	Time of Day: 1:00 Activity: Science project Grouping: Whole class, Small group		
Time	**Antecedent**	**Behaviour**	**Consequence**
1:00	Teacher giving directions, students in groups at tables	Attentive	None
1:10	4 students working on poster, reading books to gather info	Jim helping others find info; suggests categories for reporting information they found	Peers say "Good idea"
1:15	Students getting paper and pencil to record info	Jim looking over shoulder, comments on diagram in book	None
1:20	Students discussing what to put on poster	Jim drawing diagram	None
1:25	Peers tell Jim to stop. "We need to do the writing first"	Jim puts materials away, wanders off	Teacher prompts to return to group
1:30	Teacher discussing with group	Jim standing and listening	None
1:40	One student agrees to work with Jim on diagram; two are working on computer getting info	Jim drawing, discussing with partner, smiling	None

Figure 5.6 Observation #3

Portage & Main Press, 2013, *Resource Teachers*, ISBN: 978-1-55379-501-8

Analysis of Observations

What did you learn about Jim and his environment?

General observations

- Time slots are broken into longer periods — good for deeper thinking, hard for kids who have difficulty sustaining attention.
- Grouping is primarily whole class, followed by individual or independent work.
- All tasks have a written component as the assessment measure.

Student-specific observations

- Jim is consistently attentive for the first 10 min of the period, then begins to shut down.
- He maintains attention longer in small-group settings or when given the option to draw.
- Shaking hand out — fine motor issues?
- Avoidance behaviours: going to washroom, talking to peer, head down, but not ever direct refusal

Given these observations, what areas do you think might be barriers for Jim?

1. It appears that sustaining attention and fine or graphomotor tasks are challenging for Jim.
2. Visual tasks appear to engage him, as do interpersonal ones.

What interventions might you try in order to support Jim, but that might also support other students; that is, if done with the whole class as in UDL, offering some possibilities for all students.

1. **Differentiate instruction:** Give Jim and other students choices of other ways to show what they know. Because Jim is strong orally and visually, give options for oral presentations and visual representations.
2. Break tasks into smaller chunks, with mental/physical stretch breaks in between.
3. Use more small group, cooperative structures — research shows this improves engagement for all kids!
4. Offer tech choices for written tasks.

Portage & Main Press, 2013, *Resource Teachers*, ISBN: 978-1-55379-501-8

There are many possibilities, but your new knowledge of the barriers the student faces and what his strengths are allows you to make appropriate choices rather than to use random trial and error. If, after we have tried ecobehavioural interventions, the student continues to struggle in significant ways, academically or in social behaviour, we begin the process of individual assessment. We are still working in Tier 2. We are not looking to diagnose and label the student; we are simply trying to get a more detailed profile of the student's learning and to determine whether small-group or individualized interventions may now be necessary. Note that "struggle" can also imply a student who is bored, under-challenged, or disengaged. Students who are gifted may also require assessment to determine their academic and social needs. Our goal is still to help each student be successful within their classroom, but they may need more intensive support to do so — the topic of the next sections.

Portage & Main Press, 2013, *Resource Teachers*, ISBN: 978-1-55379-501-8

Section Three

Individualized Assessment for Tier 2 and Tier 3 Supports

Portage & Main Press, 2013, *Resource Teachers*, ISBN: 978-1-55379-501-8

Chapter 6
Types of Individual Assessment in Tier 2 and Tier 3

Key terms and concepts
- categorical models
- ability
- achievement
- process
- neurocognitive
- curriculum-based assessment
- normed/standardized assessment
- normal curve
- standard scores
- percentiles

Essential understandings
- Educational assessments can be divided into **four types**: ability, achievement, neurocognitive, and process assessments.
- Educational assessments can be further divided into **three levels** — A, B, and C.
- Level A tests are the educational assessments used in classrooms, such as curriculum-based assessments (e.g., a math test), interviews, surveys, and individual conferences.
- Level B or C tests are the normed/standardized educational assessments administered by specialists (e.g., trained resource teachers, speech pathologists, psychologists).

Until recently, most educational systems agreed that the process for assessing and identifying students in need of intervention should flow through a communication channel that moves from the classroom teacher's concern to assessment and intervention or remediation delivered by a special education teacher/resource teacher, to referral to a psychologist or medical doctor for formal evaluation and diagnosis. However, new models suggest a more flexible, dynamic assessment process that is based on a student's response to intervention (RTI, chapter 3) and minimizes the need for labelling and categorization. I outline the traditional model in this chapter, and consider how the two might be used in combination to support struggling learners.

Categories of Funding Models

In most provinces and states, the ministries or departments of education use a model for funding that categorizes children according to their abilities, needs, and medical status. The funding is tied to the level of a student's need, based on the assumptions made about different categories (e.g., within the autism spectrum).

Portage & Main Press, 2013, *Resource Teachers*, ISBN: 978-1-55379-501-8

Types of Assessment

- **Curriculum-based assessments** are the informal classroom assessments such as teacher evaluations of students' learning — reading inventories, portfolios, classroom work, and similar products — throughout a particular term or unit of study.

- **Standardized tests** are those that have been "normed" on a population, which means that the test was presented to a large number of students of a particular age (demographic) and, from the results, the average number of correct answers for that demographic was determined. For example, when 1,000 grade 3 students write a math test with 100 questions and the average number of correct answers is 35/100, then students in grade 3 who get 35 correct are said to be "average." The student who gets 20 correct is "below average," and the one who gets 45 correct is "above average." Such tests are then considered to have been "normed" because the students are being compared to what is normal for their age and grade, or "standardized" because students are being compared to a standard that has been developed based on the norms.

Three Levels of Assessment

1. **Level A tests** are curriculum-based and performance-based assessments, and they are not normed or standardized. This level includes classroom tests related to the specifics of a discipline: students' work samples, checklists, interviews, auditions, and similar activities.

2. **Level B tests** are standardized or normed. Examples of these tests of achievement, creativity, and cognition are WIAT (Wechsler Individual Achievement Test), PIAT (Peabody Individual Achievement Test), Woodcock-Johnson Tests of Cognitive Abilities, PPVT (Peabody Picture Vocabulary Test), KBIT-2 (Kaufman Brief Intelligence Test, Second Edition), CCAT (Canadian Cognitive Abilities Test), KeyMath3™ Diagnostic Assessment, and similar ones. These tests have to be administered by a resource teacher who has completed a specialized course in assessment and has been specifically trained in administering each test.

3. **Level C tests** are standardized tests such as IQ tests like the WISC (Wechsler Intelligence Scale for Children) or Stanford-Binet Intelligence Scales that have to be administered by an educational psychologist.

Most provinces agree that all three levels of testing are necessary for diagnostic purposes, while only levels A and B are necessary for programming purposes. Most, therefore, also agree that a student's learning profile should be built from multiple sources of information; that is, samples of classroom work, classroom observations, interviews, and specialized assessments completed by teachers,

Portage & Main Press, 2013, *Resource Teachers*, ISBN: 978-1-55379-501-8

parents, students, and specialists. The province of Manitoba's policy statement (2006) on the evaluation process is representative:

> Student assessment may take the form of teacher observation, portfolios, outcome rubrics, classroom testing and provincial assessments. For some students, where indicated, specialized assessments may be needed. Assessment methods should be appropriate for and compatible with the purpose and context of the assessment.
>
> School divisions shall:
>
> 1. Use the information gathered by the classroom teacher as the first source of information regarding student learning
> 2. Use assessment results to guide programming decisions for the student
> 3. Ensure qualified professionals who are designated by the school board or the principal conduct specialized assessments, interpret results, follow principles of fair assessment practices and provide parents and classroom teachers with programming recommendations
> 4. Use qualified professionals and other service providers and involve parents to complete specialized assessments when appropriate
> 5. Ensure that school teams, including parents when possible, are responsible for developing student-specific outcomes where indicated by the assessment process.
>
> (*Standards for Student Services* 2006, p.13)

Other provinces have similar policies; for example, Alberta's policy states:

> School boards must:
>
> 1. use a number of assessment strategies and data to determine eligibility for special education programming and services
> 2. report results of assessments to parents, teachers and others involved with students' programming
> 3. use results of assessments to make decisions, develop Individualized Program Plans (IPPs), assign support services and/or determine adapted or modified programming for students
> 4. use assessment data to develop, implement and evaluate the effectiveness of programming and services provided to students with special education needs.
>
> Specialized assessment
>
> School boards must:
>
> 1. have written procedures for referral of students requiring specialized assessment
> 2. base referrals on a variety of indicators such as:
>   - screening procedures
>   - teacher assessment and observation

Portage & Main Press, 2013, *Resource Teachers*, ISBN: 978-1-55379-501-8

- parent information
- previous assessments

3. obtain parents' written informed consent for specialized assessment or referral
4. use qualified professionals to conduct specialized assessments, interpret results, and provide program recommendations to parents, teachers and others involved with students' programming
5. work collaboratively, when appropriate, with other service providers and/or appropriate professionals to complete the specialized assessments
6. complete, when required, specialized assessments within a reasonable time (recommended guideline is within eight weeks unless there are extenuating circumstances) from the date of written referral including completion of a written report
7. follow the expectations outlined in use a number of assessment strategies and data to determine eligibility for special education programming and services Learning's Standards for Psycho-educational Assessment and by the standards and guidelines set by professional organizations for their members.

(*Standards for Special Education* 2004)

Assessments for Education Grouped into Four Subtypes

1. **Ability**
   Measures a child's potential for learning and achievement through IQ tests:
   - Level C ability tests include Wechsler Intelligence Scale for Children (WISC), Wechsler Physical Symptom Inventory (WPSI), Stanford-Binet Intelligence Scales.
   - Level B ability tests include Kaufman Brief Intelligence Test, Second Edition (KBIT-2), Test of Nonverbal Intelligences (TONI), Peabody Picture Vocabulary Test (PPVT), Canadian Cognitive Abilities Test (CCAT), Naglieri Nonverbal Ability Test (NNAT), Woodcock-Johnson Tests of Cognitive Abilities.

2. **Achievement**
   Measures what a child has already achieved or learned, e.g., standardized subject-specific tests, or curriculum-based subject-specific tests:

The statements that follow describe the consensus across North America:

1. Student assessments should come from multiple sources (parents, students, teachers, clinicians).
2. Student assessments should move from classroom-based, to specialized, as necessary, but they should not jump straight to Level C.
3. Parents must be involved, and debriefed.
4. Student assessments should be used for programming, not strictly for labelling and funding.

Portage & Main Press, 2013, *Resource Teachers*, ISBN: 978-1-55379-501-8

- Level B tests include Woodcock Johnson, Wechsler Individual Achievement Test (WIAT), Peabody Individual Achievement Test (PIAT), Kaufman Test of Educational Achievement (KTEA), KeyMath™ Diagnostic Assessment
  - Level A tests are any curriculum-based tests
3. **Neurocognitive**
   Measures processes such as memory and attention, and are usually administered by doctors
   - Conners tests for ADHD, tests of working memory
4. **Process**
   - The Learning Potential Assessment Device (LPAD) evaluates a child's learning style and potential to achieve in a mediated environment; rarely used

How Test Scores Are Measured and Reported

Standardized test reports are based on a statistical model, the normal curve. The normal curve measures the range of values seen within the human population for any continuous variable (i.e., height, weight, and IQ). For instance, the average height for a woman might be from 5'3" to 5'6". Looking at the curve, we see that 68.26% of the population would be expected to fall within this range; 13.59% would be 2 or 3 inches above or below the mean, and only about 2% of women would have a height below 5' or above 5'9".

A continuous variable can have an infinite number of different values between two given points.

In Figure 6.1, the normal curve is applied to IQ scores on the Stanford-Binet IQ test. The curve would be the same, however, for all tests. Note that the "average" range is between 85 and 115 and that 68.26% of the population fall into this range; 13.59% are 15 points above (between 116 and 131) and the same percentage are between 69 and 84; 2.27% of the population are below 68 and the same percentage are above 133.

Two types of scores can be determined from a normal curve:

1. **Standard Scores (SS)**
   a. Standard scores allow everyone to communicate clearly. You might not know that 35 out of 100 was average for a grade 3 student on the math test described earlier. However, if you see that the student has a standard score of 100 on any standardized test, you know the score is average, because average falls between 85 and 115.
   b. A student in grade 3 who scored 35 on the math test, and thus is average, would have a standard score of 100. A woman with a height of 5'4.5" would also have a standard score of 100.

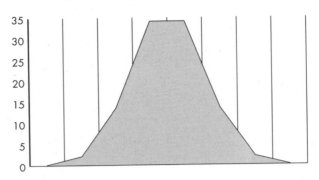

NORMAL CURVE AND THE STANFORD-BINET IQ SCORES

Percentage of cases under portions of the normal curve	0.13%	2.14%	13.59%	34.13%	34.13%	13.59%	2.14%	0.13%
Cumulative percentages		0.1%	2.3% 2%	15.9% 16%	50.0% 50%	84.1% 84%	97.7% 98%	99.9%
Stanford-Binet IQs		52	68	84	100	116	132	148

Figure 6.1 Normal curve for IQ Scores, Stanford-Binet

2. **Percentiles**
   a. A percentile indicates where a student's score falls relative to their peers of the same age; e.g., a student in the 70th percentile scored higher on the test than 70% of their peers, and lower than 30%.
   b. The 50th percentile is the same as a standard score of 100. It means average.

Blending the Traditional and RTI Models

In general, educators focus on ability tests (IQ) and achievement tests (reading level, math level) to determine their students' learning profiles. The traditional models focused on diagnostic testing. However, if we want to assess students for the purpose of devising a program, then the neurocognitive tests are important to figure out *why* a student's learning is delayed, not just that it *is* delayed. When a resource teacher receives a report that a student is reading at level x, he or she also needs to know whether that reading level is a result of difficulties with processing language or with visual memory in order to recommend the right intervention. A student who has difficulties processing language is more likely to learn to read using a sight word approach because breaking a new word into phonemes will be challenging. In contrast, the student with visual memory difficulties may struggle with sight words, but be able to respond to a phonemic awareness intervention. Resource teachers must know where the breakdown occurs for the student in order to guide decisions for programming.

Portage & Main Press, 2013, *Resource Teachers*, ISBN: 978-1-55379-501-8

Similarly, we must consider the particular area in which a student shows one or more advanced abilities. We need to explore "ceiling tests" (testing to see to what extent a student is beyond grade level, just as we do for students who are below grade level) to determine the student's instructional level and whether there are gaps between their rote skills and their comprehension, or between the content subjects, and so on.

It is possible to combine the two assessments. By first building a learning profile from assessments of students' learning challenges and strengths, we gain a big picture of the barriers — and the possible ramps over the barriers. From this profile, we want to assess whether the student has a more significant disability or gift and to refer that student for further testing. This process is recommended by many education departments both in Canada and in other countries. Ontario's *Individual Education Plan* (1998) sets out the steps for consideration and development of an IEP.

1. **Phase 1: Gather Information**
   a. Review file
   b. Conduct interviews and observations
   c. Analyze student's portfolio
   d. Test, as needed
2. **Phase 2: Set the Direction**
   a. Establish a collaborative team
   b. Define roles
3. **Phase 3: Develop the IEP**
   a. Identify strengths and needs
   b. Identify goals and expectations
   c. Determine strategies and resources
   d. Plan the transition
   e. Monitor the timeline
4. **Phase 4: Implement the IEP**
   a. Share the IEP with all team members
   b. Implement the IEP
   c. Evaluate the student's progress and the success of strategies implemented
   d. Adjust goals, expectations, and strategies — as necessary
5. **Phase 5: Review and Update**
   < www.edu.gov.on.ca/eng/general/elemsec/speced/guide/resource/iepresguid.pdf >

We have already discussed Phase 2 because in UDL we start with the team. We will now look at how the rest of these phases can be done from a UDL perspective.

Portage & Main Press, 2013, *Resource Teachers*, ISBN: 978-1-55379-501-8

Chapter 7
Gathering Information and Building Learning Profiles

Key terms and concepts
- file review
- talent development
- remediation
- overview assessments
- specific assessments

Essential understandings
- All students have relative strengths and challenges in neurodevelopmental constructs, but a significant challenge can lead to a learning disability.
- Assessment needs to follow a process in which we examine what we already know, and then plan assessments to confirm or reject this information, and fill in any gaps to give us a full picture of a student's learning profile.
- It is important to get a "big picture" of a student's learning profile.
- Specific assessments allow us to get detailed information about students' strengths and challenges.

The human brain is still a mystery to us. Although we have learned a great deal in the last decades, we still have so much more to learn. When a student finds learning challenging, assessment becomes detective work. We have to make inferences, using clues gathered through observation, conferencing, testing, and portfolio analysis about where a student's strengths and challenges lie. This is a creative, intuitive, and analytical process — and should be enjoyable for both student and teacher as we discover this student's kind of mind. We look for clues about a student's strengths and challenges that can guide our decisions about testing. How do we decide which of the many possible assessments to use? The Three-Block Model of UDL differs significantly from what is commonly used in the field. Most traditional assessment practices are based on what a student cannot do, even when they claim to support a "strengths-based approach" to learning. Often, though, when that student's strengths are listed on the front page of an IEP, nothing is done with them. All goals set out in the subsequent pages focus on the remediation of the weakness. On the rare occasion when strengths are used, it is to overcome the weaknesses, which serves only to tie the student's affinities to what they cannot do,

Portage & Main Press, 2013, *Resource Teachers*, ISBN: 978-1-55379-501-8

and often reduces their engagement in these talents. For instance, teachers will "let a student draw before they write." If the student does not like writing, but learns that every time they draw they will then be expected to write, they soon stop enjoying drawing.

In the Three-Block Model of UDL, we look for opportunities to develop students' talents. We actively seek to develop students' strengths, not just use them to remediate weaknesses. But think about that: If someone had said to Mozart, "You're good enough at music. We need to work on your spelling," there would be no Mozart! Obviously, we must not ignore areas of challenge: rather, we must find a balance between working with them on the areas of learning that they find challenging and letting them feel successful in school. Too often in current practice, we remove students from doing what they enjoy — or at least can do — to make them spend more time on the things they cannot do such as reading, writing, or math. Then we wonder why they start hating school, or disengaging — why they begin to think of themselves as stupid.

We must ensure that students spend some time in school doing what they love and what they are good at — which gives them an opportunity to look smart or successful in front of their peers, and to develop the skills they can use in their future careers. After all, a student who is a talented in art but has a learning disability might one day become a graphic designer or an architect — if we allow them to develop their talents in visual perception and representation and don't destroy their self-esteem in the meantime. Today, all universities offer services to students with a disability; for example, students can sit oral exams instead of writing exams or have someone scribe their responses. Similarly, in elementary and secondary levels, students should be allowed to develop the skills that will allow them to overcome their disability.

Many provinces recognize this in policy, but not always in practice. In Quebec, the ministry's IEP planning document (2004) states:

> School staff are encouraged to take into consideration all aspects of a student's situation, and to focus on his or her strengths and the resources of the school in order to help him or her to progress. The document also underlines the need to make the individualized education plan part of a creative approach to problem solving that demands teamwork and an open-minded attitude in all involved. (*Individualized Education Plans: Helping Students Achieve Success, Reference Framework for the Establishment of Individual Education Plans*, 2004, Quebec Ministry of Education, Recreation and Sports)

Sounds good, doesn't it? However, this document and many others continue by suggesting IEPs focus on the adaptations or modifications, that is, what the student cannot do and no mention of what the student can do. Only the gifted students are recognized as needing goals based on their strengths because enrichment is a form of adaptation — and adaptation of a curriculum is what teachers know how to do.

I believe that any policy focused on adaptation of the curriculum is a fundamental mistake — an IEP should be truly individualized, that is, focused on

Portage & Main Press, 2013, *Resource Teachers*, ISBN: 978-1-55379-501-8

the success and inclusion of an individual student and balancing that student's IEP with as many opportunities for success in what they do know as in sessions focused on learning what they do not know. At the same time, we also want to know in what area, and why, a student struggles. The students who are struggling in a particular subject or skill, such as reading or math, are the ones who are referred to resource teachers by their classroom teachers. RTs want to know not only to what extent the student is falling behind, but also the reasons why. Is the student struggling with writing because of challenges with fine motor skills, working memory, language recall, or something else? If a student appears to be struggling with memory, we would want to conduct assessments of memory. If they appear to have strength in visual-spatial activities, we would want to assess that area to confirm whether it's a talent to be developed.

File Reviews and Work Samples: The Process

Once involved, the RT begins by asking the classroom teacher for samples of the student's work and that teacher's observations about the student's performance and participation for clues about strengths and challenges in the student's learning. As resource teachers, we can use this information to plan our assessment, while refraining from drawing any conclusions until we have actually worked with the student ourselves.

Step 1: File Summaries

Look for any past test results, medical records, and so on. Read report cards, looking for indicators of strengths and challenges, comments or observations repeated over the years (e.g., attentional challenges), and acquisition of learning basics (e.g., when student learned to read). For example, repeated observations that "Johnny is working on remembering his math facts" or "Johnny is working on bringing all his materials to class" (i.e., he doesn't remember routines) suggests that you might need to conduct an assessment of memory.

Step 2: Portfolio Analysis

Use the samples of the student 's work in the file, and look for indicators of strengths and challenges as clues about where the breakdowns might lie. As an example, on a 3-page math test, you might note that the student's answers are all correct on page 1, but the error rate increases on page 2 and again on page 3, and you consider this an indication that the student has attentional challenges. Look also for any obvious talents that the teaching team might help the student develop. Assess the context in which the work samples were completed: Is it a written piece? When was it completed? What were the instructions? Was any assistance provided?

Portage & Main Press, 2013, *Resource Teachers*, ISBN: 978-1-55379-501-8

Try This

Review these two report cards for Jim Doe, the grade 7 student described in chapter 5. What do you notice about the comments? Are there clues here?

Student Name: Jim Doe   Date: _____

Please read, sign, and return this report to school with your child. If you would like to discuss any part of the report,

_____

_____.

Mid-term Grade:		Comments
B	Language Arts	Jim is able to read advanced level novels, and to synthesize the themes and deeper meanings in them. Jim struggles to express his thinking in writing; he rushes through and writes short, simple sentences.
C+	Math	Jim is able to solve complex, applied mathematical problems working with a group. However, his tests and assignments have many computation errors. He needs to check over his work.
A	Social Studies	This is Jim's greatest strength; he is able to analyze social and historical issues with maturity beyond his years, and works well with visuals like maps. Jim requires adaptations for writing, however.
B	Science	Jim has advanced conceptual understanding in science, though he is not as engaged in it as he is with social studies. He was late with several assignments, and did not hand in two at all.
C+	Foreign Language	Jim understands both French and English fully, but has some difficulty expressing himself, and remembering to organize his ideas.
B	Art	Jim works well when exploring media, interpreting imagery, and appreciating artistic techniques, however, he at times struggles to apply these skills.
A	Music	Jim is a very talented musician, both vocally and instrumentally. He composes his own music, plays several instruments, and is a trained vocalist.
C	Physical Education	Jim often appears disengaged in PE; he daydreams and misses his turn or role in games. Jim lacks coordination and strength, and would benefit from extracurricular sports.

Parent/Guardian Signature: _____ Date: _____

Portage & Main Press, 2013, *Resource Teachers*, ISBN: 978-1-55379-501-8

Student Progress Report: Jim Doe
123 Middle School   Term 3
Grade: 7   Div: 8   June 2004

Personal Intelligences (Inter- and Intra-personal, Existentialist Intelligences)

Jim says: "I get along well with everyone. I know my strengths and my challenges."

Teachers say: "Jim is right, he is a great friend to everyone. Throughout the term, he has contributed significantly to our class meetings and discussions. When Jim is focused, he is a deep thinker and poses high-level questions. We appreciate his ability to help his group mates make sense of complex ideas."

Science (Naturalist Intelligence)

Jim says: "I learned about ecosystems and the effects we are having on them. My challenge is researching, but I think I'm meeting expectations."

Teachers say: "This term we have studied the natural resources involved in the development of Steveston, BC, particularly the fishing industry and the use of the waterways. Jim's sensitivity extends to his reflections on nature and environmental issues. He is able to understand how communities live off the natural resources of their surroundings, and the balance required for interdependence."

English Language Arts (Verbal-Linguistic Intelligence)

Jim says: "I am trying to get better. I have been reading since kindergarten, but my challenge is writing!"

Teachers say: "Jim's right, he has worked hard this term on improving his written expression. Although this is something that challenges Jim, he definitely has the ideas and vocabulary to express himself effectively. Jim tends to tire easily but, when prompted, contributes to group work. His reading is exceeding expectations, and this is something that Jim is very proud of. He takes great pleasure out of reading and is proud of his accomplishments in this area."

Physical Education (Bodily-Kinesthetic Intelligence)

Jim says: "What can I say – I'm just not good at sports or building. I can act, though."

Teachers say: "Jim has great skill in the performing arts, including drama and music. In PE, Jim struggles with coordination and balance; his fine-motor skills in drawing and printing are also a challenge for him."

Art (Visual-Spatial Intelligence)

Jim says: "I like art, and I like looking at maps, photographs, and videos. My strength is shading, my challenge is drawing, but I think I am meeting expectations."

Teachers say: "Although this is not Jim's favourite subject, he has developed a new-found interest in it. Jim did a great job of creating props for the plays that his group performed and took pride in many of the miniature 3-D models for our Steveston maps. Jim learns well through visuals, and he can represent concepts symbolically."

Band (Musical-Rhythmic Intelligence)

Jim says: "I play in two bands, and sing in the Boys Choir. I have just started composing — this is definitely my strength, and my future."

Teachers say: "Jim is an exceptionally talented musician, and excels at expressing himself musically both vocally and instrumentally. He has rhythm and can move to the music although he is often a little shy in doing so. His Steveston group created and performed a fantastic chant about Steveston, and added sound effects and acting roles."

Math (Logical-Mathematical Intelligence)

Jim says: "Math is not really my favourite — it's hard for me to remember all the steps. I like geometry, though. I think I am meeting expectations."

Teachers say: "Jim has fully met the expectations for numeracy at his grade level. He understands the concepts in numeracy and can problem solve. At times, Jim struggles with computation, as he forgets steps in processes such as long division or solving an algebraic equation. He often uses mental math to arrive at a correct answer quickly, and he can use more than one strategy when problem solving."

Jim is a deep thinker and enriches the learning of his classmates. He needs to continue to work on managing his concentration, energy, and materials.

Portage & Main Press, 2013, *Resource Teachers*, ISBN: 978-1-55379-501-8

Analysis

Looking at the report cards, we can see that:

1. Jim was an early reader.
2. Jim is highly musical and visual.
3. Jim asks deep questions and seeks knowledge.
4. Jim struggles to maintain attention.
5. Jim has difficulty with motor coordination.

Developing Assessment Plans

Consulting with teachers, parents, and students and conducting a file review and portfolio analysis give us a first snapshot of how the student learns best, and what aspects of learning they find challenging. We can now pose some educated questions about Jim's learning profile. This is an "assessment for learning" process, as we seek to determine what Jim knows and can do, where he is struggling and why, and what we need to teach him. We ask ourselves questions such as:

What do we know about the student?

What can the student do well?

How best does the student learn?

What is challenging for them?

What do we still need to know about the student in order to guide the instruction?

Often one assessment will lead to questions, then further assessment. That's okay — like a detective, we follow the evidence. It is common to begin by suspecting that attention is an issue, and then realize that memory is a more significant factor. It's important to begin with a plan, but we must be open to changing it. With Jim as our example, we know we want to assess his attention, language, motor skills, visual-spatial abilities, existential abilities, higher-order cognition, and musical abilities.

We also want to use multiple sources. It is important to talk to Jim, his parents, and his teachers about these areas of his learning and perhaps about other areas if questions arise as we proceed. Before we work directly with the student, it is important to gather materials and consider time factors. How long will these assessments take? How long is this student's attention span? Any assessments might need to be conducted in chunks, but the normed tests cannot be stopped in the middle, so we must plan the timeframe to complete one test at a time. No single assessment tells us everything, nor does one assessor!

Portage & Main Press, 2013, *Resource Teachers*, ISBN: 978-1-55379-501-8

Try This

Examine the two samples of Jim's classwork. Describe what you see and can infer from the similarities and differences.

May 3

The 'Death man

I now a man that set and fed the birds I yell at him I bont say an drib but he awep say there Wiko me some day 2 Weeks Later he was never agoin a so i think he gao whit a bird to hevan.

The Deaf Man

I know a man that sat and fed the birds

I yelled at him " I don't see any birds"

But he always said "They will come

someday"

Two weeks later

He was never there again

So I think he's gone with the birds

To Heaven

Analysis of Observations

Notice the difference between what Jim can do in writing, and what he can do using technology. There is very sophisticated imagery and theme here, but also evidence of challenges with sequencing. At this point, we have first impressions of what Jim's challenges and barriers might be and where his strengths lie. This knowledge allows us to formulate a plan for assessment, to either confirm or reject our hypotheses, and fill in with what we might have overlooked. From the files and portfolio, we note:

Jim's strengths	Jim's challenges
visual-spatial musical-rhythmic existential higher-order cognition social-cognition	sustaining attention / mental energy neuromotor function

We don't yet know much about Jim's language-processing, his memory, or his general health, so we may want to screen for these as well. For now, it is time to select the Level A and Level B assessments we can do to acquire more details.

Level A Assessments

Level A assessments are informal, yet they can be the most informative. Focus on:

- family context
- social, emotional, and behavioural realms
- cognitive processing
- literacy
- numeracy
- known areas of strength and of challenge

Of the different types of Level A assessment, the most useful is personal observation of the student in their natural context — in the class, on the playground, and so on. It helps to have several people observe, and to ask others about their observations in order to develop a big picture of the student's learning and behaviour. You are looking for patterns, as in the ecobehavioural assessment. When, where, with whom, and in what tasks does the student excel and seem happy? When, where, with whom, and in what tasks does the student struggle?

- Observe students in a variety of contexts
- Observe students in focused contexts (i.e., where their strengths and challenges will likely show)

Portage & Main Press, 2013, *Resource Teachers*, ISBN: 978-1-55379-501-8

- Observe for specifics (e.g., attention, higher-order cognition)
- Look for the big picture — strengths and challenges

Gather further information through interviews and surveys like the survey of multiple intelligences and learning styles. Interest inventories allow us to hear directly from the students as to how they see themselves, which also helps build rapport as they share themselves with us. A teacher can devise such an interest inventory simply based on the eight neurodevelopmental constructs (see pp. 43–47).

TtD Appendix

- Ask the students such questions as:
  - Do you have a good memory or do you forget things a lot?
  - Do you learn well by listening?
  - How organized are you?
  - Some students have a hard time when teachers talk fast. Does that happen for you?
  - Some students are really good at _____. Is that true for you?
- When exploring memory, teachers can use simple ways such as the card game Memory to test neurodevelopmental constructs with a student.
- Another simple assessment of working memory: Say that you will read three sentences and, when finished, you will ask them to repeat the first sentence. (The student has to hold the first sentence in mind while listening to the next two sentences).
- A simple test of visual memory: Show the student five pictures. Turn the pictures over. Ask the student what was in them.
- To observe a student's ability to follow multi-step directions, specify a sequence of actions (e.g., stand up, turn around, touch your toes, clap your hands) for the student to do when you say "Go." If the student performs the action, but out of sequence, sequential ordering may be an issue. As a result, the student is likely struggling to initiate and complete tasks because they cannot sort out the steps they need to take. If the student cannot remember the instructions, or asks you to repeat the instructions more than one time, then memory is the issue and the student will experience difficulty following auditory instructions in class.

The point here is that you do not need standardized tests to assess a student's profile. You can use everyday tasks to observe where the breakdowns occur.

Spotlight

Many informal surveys and scales available on the Internet are attentional screens, scales of belonging, and social emotional well-being. To find several on multiple intelligences, including an MI survey, try <surfaquarium.com>. In addition, the SELF research institute has scales of self-concept and belonging.

Assessments Based on Curriculum

Curriculum-based assessments are most familiar to teachers: assessing a writing sample, completing running records, recording performance in class in areas of concern, examining the student's artwork and projects. These are all valuable and valid measures. Portfolio samples can also contribute to the ecobehavioural assessment. For a larger picture of the student's learning, ask: What did we not have? What did we not see? We may have a writing sample, but do we know how much help the student had to complete it? If not, we might bring the student in and ask for an unsupported writing sample, so we can see what the student is able to do independently. Together, our observations both of what a student can do in a one-to-one assessment and of what they can do in class tell us a lot about a student's learning processes. For example, if a student writes more fluently and powerfully in a one-to-one situation than in their classroom, then distractibility might be the issue. If the writing they produce in the classroom is better, then perhaps the student benefits from opportunities to dialogue with other students, or even when just feeling "the buzz" in the room. A student who has challenges with attentional control will find the classroom distracting, but a student who struggles to maintain mental energy might remain alert longer with some sensory stimulation.

Analyzing Level A assessments

Look for gaps in the student's file of materials. Is there a difference between reading comprehension and listening comprehension? What does an oral re-telling reveal that a written piece doesn't? Take care to consider the student's strengths and challenges (achievement and neurodevelopmental) over a range of developmental activities (academic, social-emotional, and behavioural).

Level A: Ability Assessments	Level A: Achievement Assessments
Problem-solving activities	Reading conference; informal reading inventories
Content and thematic maturity in art, music, humour, discussions, and writing	Projects, illustrations, artifacts that the student has created
MI survey	Writing sample
Neurodevelopmental screen	Math work
Moral dilemmas	Social Responsibility Performance Standards (BC), and other social and emotional scales

Figure 7.1 Types of Level A assessments

Portage & Main Press, 2013, *Resource Teachers*, ISBN: 978-1-55379-501-8

Analyzing Level B assessments

Use Level B assessments to support and add detail to your findings during your Level A assessment. Using a range of tests that cover both ability and achievement allows you to see whether the student is achieving to potential.

Level B: Ability Assessments	Level B: Achievement Assessments
Kaufmann Brief Intelligence Test (KBIT)	Peabody Individual Achievement Test (PIAT)
Test of Nonverbal Intelligence (TONI)	Wechsler Individual Achievement Tests (WIAT)
Woodcock-Johnson Tests of Cognitive Abilities	Woodcock-Johnson Tests of Achievement
Canadian Cognitive Abilities Test (CCAT)	Specific tests: • KeyMath • Test of Written Language (TOWL)
Naglieri Nonverbal Ability Test (NNAT)	Marsh Self-Description Questionnaire
	Test of Pragmatic Language (TOPL) or other social language and skills assessments

Figure 7.2 Types of Level B assessments

Portage & Main Press, 2013, *Resource Teachers*, ISBN: 978-1-55379-501-8

Try This

Which tests would you select for Jim?

Construct	Level A	Level B
Higher-order cognition	Problem solving activities Logic problems	Ability assessments: KBIT-2 TONI
Social cognition	Observations, behavioural records Informal scales related to belonging, social skills, empathy BC Performance Standards for Social Responsibility	Social Skills Improvement System (SSIS) Rating Scales Facial Expressions of Emotional Stimuli and Tests (Ekman)
Attention	Observations – time sampling of on/off task Concentration Cockpit	Conners (ADHD)
Language	Think-Aloud Story telling Phonemic awareness	PPVT EPVT
Memory	Retelling a story Multi-step directions Sentence recall Picture recall	Woodcock-Johnson
Temporal-sequential	Sequencing pictures Story retelling Following directions	
Spatial ordering	Figure-ground assessments Visual memory Following directions (e.g., "When I say go, draw a circle. On top of the circle place a triangle. Beside the circle draw an arrow.") Perspective tests (e.g. show the student an item that is different on each side. Let them look at all sides, then show them one, and ask them what they think you see, sitting on the opposite side)	Woodcock-Johnson
Neuromotor	OT consult Pencil grip Hand-eye coordination Sewing cards	Clinical Assessment of Writing Bruininks-Oseretsky Test of Motor Proficiency, Second Edition (BOT-2)

Figure 7.3 Table of Level A and Level B tests

Portage & Main Press, 2013, *Resource Teachers*, ISBN: 978-1-55379-501-8

Analysis of Choices

Jim has appeared to be an existential thinker with strength in higher-order cognition, so we want figure out where Jim's ability actually lies. We could conduct a Level B ability test such as the Kaufmann Brief Intelligence Test (KBIT), the results of which can provide a measure of both verbal and nonverbal ability, that is, visual reasoning. An interest inventory or the MI survey also could confirm for us whether Jim is as inspired by music and visual learning as his mom believes.

We want a greater awareness of Jim's challenges because we are wondering about attention. The Concentration Cockpit (available from the All Kinds of Minds Institute <www.allkindsofminds.org>) is one attention screen that explores a person's ability to sustain attention, not just hyperactivity and impulsivity, which do not seem to be his issues. We also wonder about his motor skills, so we might find it useful a) to consult with an occupational therapist, b) to observe Jim's pencil grip when writing, c) to observe his abilities in physical education class, and d) to administer neuromotor tests.

Finally, we will want to administer achievement tests that explore writing fluency and the memory aspects of writing. Reading inventories and similar assessments can all be helpful in determining whether Jim's challenges really affect his learning, and to what degree.

Now that we know what we want to know and how we are going to assess it, we are ready to bring Jim in and begin conducting assessments. In the next chapter, we will discuss how to conduct Level A and Level B assessments.

Portage & Main Press, 2013, *Resource Teachers*, ISBN: 978-1-55379-501-8

Chapter 8

Gathering Information for Levels A and B Assessments

Key terms and concepts
- basal levels
- ceiling levels
- confidence intervals
- raw scores

Essential understandings
- Level A assessments are flexible and creative.
- Level B assessments require a standardized protocol for administering them and scoring them.

Assessment is always challenging — even at the classroom level. How do we know what a student knows and understands? How do we determine why that student finds a skill or concept challenging to master? The steps necessary in building a learning profile take time, but it's important that all resource teachers know how to do such assessments. However, the intention of "response to intervention" (RTI) and ecobehavioural assessment is to reduce the number of students requiring in-depth assessment profiles. Both classroom teachers and resource teachers can initiate the actions described in the three tiers of RTI and in ecobehavioural assessment. Of course, more specialized assessments may be required for some struggling students in order to determine in greater detail where the student's strengths lie, where the breakdowns in the neurodevelopmental processes may be occurring, and what programming could be helpful.

Conducting Assessments

When the student is anxious or does not trust the interviewer, the results of any assessments will not be valid. A resource teacher who does not know the student must first establish some rapport by chatting. Even when teachers do have a relationship with the student being assessed, it's important that the student feel at ease about the reason for the meeting or interview. A parent or classroom teacher who uses the word "test" may raise the student's anxiety immediately.

Portage & Main Press, 2013, *Resource Teachers*, ISBN: 978-1-55379-501-8

Beginning an Assessment

1. Greet the student and chat lightly initially.

2. Ask the student: "Do you know why you were asked to meet with me?"

3. Build on prior discussions of the multiple intelligences to demystify the brain's functioning for the student. Explain that all people have strengths and challenges, and that their teachers want to know how best to teach each student.

4. One way to do this is to talk to students about the brain, as perhaps in Lesson 3, page 37, in *Teaching to Diversity*. Another way is describe the brain as "being like a city — the city has roads that come in to the city and go out, and each road carries different types of information." Draw a brain with nine roads coming in and out. Label each with one of the intelligences. Tell the students that for all of us, some of these roads are six-lane highways and some are two-lane gravel roads. Tell them about your roads. For instance, I could say that I learn well through verbal-linguistic roads but not through visual-spatial or bodily kinesthetic roads. Ask which ones they think are their "highways" and which are their "gravel roads."

   However you explain this, be sure the student understands that there are ways in which they learn well and ways that are challenging for them, and that's okay.

5. Explain some of the activities that the students will do, and give them some choice as to how to begin. Let them know that some activities will be in their areas of strength and might feel easy for them, and other activities will be in their areas of challenge and might be difficult for them. Tell them you would like them to give their best on each activity, so that you can see what they can do and how you can best support them.

During Level A

1. Chat, probe, be creative.

2. Remember, you don't need formal tests.

   a. Wondering about their language processing? Tell the student a story, and ask them to retell it to you. Note that memory plays a role here, too.

   b. Wondering about their ability to focus and maintain focus? Start the student on an activity, then start moving some papers around. Does the child get distracted? For how long?

3. Compare listening to reading, and writing to speaking.

   a. Have the student write a story, then have them tell you a story later in the assessment. Is there a significant difference in the content? in the detail? If so, then writing is the issue, not expressive language. If they struggle both orally and in writing, then expressive language, sequencing, or higher-order cognition underlies their challenge.

b. Read a passage to them, then have them read one to you. Is there a difference in their comprehension? If so, then decoding or working memory might be an issue (because it takes working memory to hold in your mind what you just read while you figure out the next sentence), not receptive language or higher-order cognition. If the student struggles with both, then the issue is not decoding but a language or cognitive issue.

4. To get a big picture of the student's capacity for learning, use overviews such as:

a. Neurocognitive checklists

b. MI Survey

c. Interviews / affinity inventories

5. Get specific details, according to your plan, about neurodevelopmental constructs using selected assessments such as:

a. Higher-order cognition

- portfolio assessment or observation of process
  - conceptual understanding
  - problem solving

b. Social cognition

- observations, behavioural records
- informal scales related to belonging, social skills, empathy
- BC Performance Standards for social responsibility

c. Attention

- observations through time-sampling of the student, both on-task and off-task
- Concentration Cockpit
- Conners ADHD Index

d. Language

- PPVT (Peabody Picture Vocabulary Test)
- think-aloud responses

- storytelling
- phonemic awareness

e. Memory

- retelling a story
- multi-step directions
- sentence recall
- picture recall

f. Temporal-sequential

- sequencing pictures
- story retelling
- following directions

g. Spatial-ordering

- figure-ground assessments
- visual memory
- following directions (e.g., "When I say Go, draw a circle. Then, place a triangle on top of the circle. Then, beside the circle, draw an arrow.")
- perspective tests (e.g., Show the student a block-like item that is different on each side. Allow time to look at all sides. Then show one side, and ask "What do you think I can see while sitting on the opposite side?"

h. Neuromotor skills

- occupational therapist (OT) consult
- pencil grip
- hand-eye coordination
- sewing cards

Also assess achievement in curricular areas — reading, writing, mathematics.

During Level B

Level B tests are standardized. Some teachers take university graduate courses or specialized training in their school divisions to acquire the qualifications to administer assessments; others acquire their expertise from the training

The point of assessment is to support students, to be aware that they might have feelings of anxiety and self-doubt. The teacher must be explicit about — and must demystify for students — both the procedures and the materials every step of the way. Ensure that students know what is about to happen, why they are being asked to participate in the process, so that they will feel a sense of success upon completion.

Portage & Main Press, 2013, *Resource Teachers*, ISBN: 978-1-55379-501-8

Of course, you will not conduct all these assessments, nor even one from each area. This list is not exhaustive, rather it is intended to give some ideas for developing a plan. Using the student's apparent strengths and challenges, pick and choose assessments that will best reveal more of what teachers need to understand about the student.

courses of the relevant publisher (see Test Instruments, p. 174). What follows, therefore, is an overview/review of the process, intended to help resource teachers understand the purpose and process of the testing and, perhaps, seek such training, but such an overview does not qualify people to administer these tests — they must take the courses and be supervised in their training.

Level B tests must be administered according to the procedures set out in the publisher's manual for a particular test because students' scores are compared with the scores of other students who took the test under the same conditions (i.e., within a specific timeframe, with specific instructions). All tests are administered one-on-one — teacher-to-student — with oral instructions.

Each Level B test has an administration procedure — the administrator's manual contains the instructions specific to the test and the students. In general, the opening script for the teacher explains the test's nature and purpose to the student. The student's age determines the starting point — the early items are for younger children. For example, if a 6-year-old starts at item 1, a 12-year-old might start at item 15, skipping what the developers of the instrument believe a student of that age could achieve. You must start the student at the point designated for their chronological age — even if you believe your student is not capable of handling the early items. Usually, an assessment has a base that the student must achieve before moving on (e.g., three correct in a row, or one set correct). If the student does not achieve that **basal level** (i.e., the items are too hard), then move the student back to an earlier starting point. When the items are too difficult for the student (e.g., three sequential items are incorrect), that becomes the **ceiling**, the point at which you stop. Each test differs in the number of items a student gets right or wrong for either basal or ceiling, but all Level B tests have a basal level and a ceiling.

To provide an example, let's imagine a test with 100 items, on which getting three items in a sequence correct is the basal level of achievement, and getting four items in a sequence wrong is the ceiling. For a student of age 13, 14, or 15, the starting point is item 15. For a student of age 10, 11, or 12, the starting point is item 10. You are to assess Jim, who is 13 years and 4 months old, so you start with item 15. Jim gets item 15 correct, but then he gets item 16 wrong. Because he has not achieved the **basal** (three items correct), you start back at item 10 then go through to item 15. If he does not get items 10, 11, and 12 correct as the basal, you go back further to the starting point for a student who is 5 or 6 years old, and so on until your student achieves the **basal** of three sequential items correct. Then, you skip items 15 and 16 (because you already administered them), and go to item 17. You will continue the items until the student gets four sequential items wrong.

Portage & Main Press, 2013, *Resource Teachers*, ISBN: 978-1-55379-501-8

During the Administration

1. Monitor the pace and duration of the test. Keep moving along, but watch for student fatigue. If the student grows tired, the results are not valid. You must provide a break after one test is done, before you resume with the next test.

2. Make note of any behavioural changes, attentional focus, and signs of stress or anxiety.

3. When administering multi-level tests, explain to the students that the test covers an age and grade range, and that they should not feel bad if they find it challenging. You can tell students the test is used from kindergarten to university, so the first items will be easy, then the items will become more challenging, but you will stop the student when the items become too difficult. We do not want students to feel like failures when they stop.

4. Encourage students to take their time, look over all the options, and make educated guesses.

5. Don't give students feedback either pro or con, but be consistently supportive.

6. Select from both ability tests and achievement tests so you can explore any gaps between potential and learning.

After Completing the Assessments

1. Ask the students whether they have any questions or concerns.

2. Be honest about what you see because the kids already know. For example, if the student asks, "How did I do?" answer, "Well, I haven't looked it all over yet, but my impression is that your mind learns better with ____ (e.g., pictures) than with ____ (e.g., words). Does that sound right to you?"

3. Consider all the pieces of the student's learning profile. Do not base decisions on one piece of assessment data.

4. Follow up with further assessments if questions remain in your mind.

Scoring Level B Tests

All standardized tests have a common process for analysis, usually detailed in the manual.

1. Calculate raw scores, usually by subtracting errors from the ceiling item.

2. Most test manuals have tables (usually organized by age or grade) that indicate the equivalent standard scores and percentiles for a student's raw score.

3. Find the tables for the age and grade of the students you have assessed.

4. Determine the standard scores and percentiles matching the raw scores.

5. If appropriate, compute the composite score.

Let's look at an example. Imagine Figure 8.1 shows the results for one student.

Item #	Answer correct? √	Item #	Answer correct? √
1		21	X
2		22	√
3		23	X
4		24	X
5		25	√
6		26	√
7		27	X
8		28	X
9		29	√
10	√	30	X
11	√	31	√
12	√	32	X
13	√	33	X
14	√	34	√
15	√	35	√
16	X	36	X
17	√	37	X
18	√	38	X
19	X	39	X
20	√	40	

Figure 8.1 Sample scoring for standardized test

The **ceiling** item is #39 (i.e., the item where you stopped the assessment). The student made 14 errors, so the raw score is 39 − 14 = 25.

Now we go to the tables in the manual (Figure 8.2 on the next page).

Jim, with a raw score of 25, has a standard score of 99 and a percentile rank of 47, which puts him in the average range (see chapter 7). The confidence interval is meant to show us the range of scores this student could fall into, because no test is perfect and the student might have gotten one more or one less on another day. We can be confident, with 90% certainty, that Jim would fall into a range from 91 to 107, in other words, the average range.

Portage & Main Press, 2013, *Resource Teachers*, ISBN: 978-1-55379-501-8

Ages 13–19			
Raw Score	Standard Score	90% Confidence Interval	Percentile Rank
30	109	100–117	73
29	107	98–115	68
28	105	96–113	63
27	103	95–111	58
26	101	93–109	53
25	99	91–107	47
24	97	89–105	42
23	95	87–104	37
22	93	85–102	32
21	91	83–100	27
20	88	80–97	21

Figure 8.2 Score equivalencies

Analyzing and Interpreting Results

No single test gives us an accurate picture of the complexity of the human mind. This is why we must gather assessment data from multiple sources. When we now sit down to look at what we have learned about the student's strengths and challenges, we have taken the following items into account: student's files with past history and data; student's work samples; interviews, surveys, and curricular assessments; Level A and B assessments of neurodevelopmental constructs; Level A and B assessments of ability and achievement.

These give us a big picture of a student's learning profile. In the scenario, Jim's receptive language tested in the average range, as shown by the score. His self-assessment indicates that he understands concepts in science and social studies, and his work samples and teachers' reports confirm this in oral discussions. We can be confident, then, that he has strength in higher-order cognition.

Although Jim passed the writing fluency test, which requires a rate of writing within 3 minutes, both he and his teacher agree that he has difficulties completing longer written pieces. He writes in simple sentences using simple vocabulary, neither of which matches his spoken abilities. On the finger succession task (a test of fine motor coordination), his was in the disabled range, indicating that he might have a problem with fine motor skills. In interviews, Jim had indicated that he has trouble with multi-step directions, which could indicate issues with working memory, language processing, or sequencing. However, his memory tests fell within the acceptable range, as did his receptive language. Thus, sequencing might be a factor here.

Portage & Main Press, 2013, *Resource Teachers*, ISBN: 978-1-55379-501-8

Try This

What do the results below from Jim's testing tell you?

1. Kaufmann Brief Intelligence Test (KBIT)
   - Verbal IQ = 75th percentile, SS = 110, above average
   - Nonverbal IQ = 95th percentile, SS = 125, superior
   - Composite IQ = 90th percentile, SS = 119, superior (invalid due to gap)
2. Peabody Picture Vocabulary Test (PPVT)
   - 47th percentile, SS = 99, average
3. Johns Basic Reading Inventory (BRI)
   - Reading level = Grade 10
4. Tests of written output
   - Alphabet task — acceptable range
   - Handwriting fluency — acceptable range
   - Narrative fluency — acceptable range
   - Expository fluency — acceptable range
   - Finger succession — disabled range
5. Tests of active working memory
   - Listening recall — acceptable range
   - Listening generate — acceptable range
6. Concentration Cockpit
   - Strengths — mood and behavioural control (impulsivity)
   - Challenges — sensory filtration and free flight (distractibility and daydreaming), arousal control (sustaining attention)
7. Neurodevelopmental constructs (self-report survey)
   - Strengths — higher-order cognition, social cognition
   - Challenges — attention, expressive language, sequencing, mood/affect (anxiety)
8. MI Survey (self-report and parent survey)
   - Strengths — musical-rhythmic, existential, intrapersonal
   - Challenges — verbal-linguistic (expressive), bodily-kinesthetic

Portage & Main Press, 2013, *Resource Teachers*, ISBN: 978-1-55379-501-8

Analysis of Assessment

In my role as an educational consultant, I prepared a report on the student Jim Doe. Review my discussion of the porfolio of Level A and B observations and test results to see how conclusions can be drawn from the varied threads.

Jennifer Katz
Educational Consultant

Educational Report

Child's Name: Jim Doe
Father's Name: John Doe
Mother's Name: Jane Doe

Child's DOB: Nov. 28, _____

History

Jim was referred for assessment by his mother, who expressed interest in knowing more about his learning strengths and challenges. Jim is in grade 7 at Mr. Smith school, where he is enrolled in the French Immersion program. On first contact by phone, Jim's mother expressed pride in Jim's verbal skills and creative thinking. At the same time, she expressed concern that Jim was experiencing difficulty in school with completing work, organizing materials, and he had begun avoiding homework assignments. Ms. Doe reported that Jim's teachers were concerned that Jim may be challenged by attentional difficulties or a written output disorder. Thus a wide array of Level A and B assessments were conducted to develop a learning profile for Jim.

Assessment Tools

Kaufmann Brief Intelligence Test (KBIT-2)
Peabody Picture Vocabulary Test [IIIA] (PPVT)
Johns Basic Reading Inventory (BRI)
Test of Written Language (TOWL)
Tests of active working memory
Views attuned
Curriculum-based assessments as well as checklists, rating scales, and interviews

Summary of Results

1) KBIT
        Verbal IQ = 75th percentile, SS = 110, Above average
        Nonverbal IQ = 95th percentile, SS = 125, Superior
        Composite IQ = 90th percentile, SS = 119, Superior (invalid due to gap)
2) PPVT 47th percentile, SS = 99, average
3) Johns BRI Reading level = Grade 10

Figure 8.3 Jim's Assessment Report

Portage & Main Press, 2013, *Resource Teachers*, ISBN: 978-1-55379-501-8

4) Tests of written output
        Alphabet task – Acceptable Range
        Handwriting Fluency – Acceptable Range
        Narrative Fluency – Acceptable Range
        Expository Fluency – Acceptable Range
        Finger Succession – *Disabled* Range
5) Tests of active working memory
        Listening Recall – Acceptable Range
        Listening Generate – Acceptable Range
** *See discussion section for further reporting of results*

Discussion of Results and Observations

Jim presented as a bright, articulate young man. He was willing and eager to please throughout the assessment, though he was highly anxious, lost concentration easily, and became fatigued quickly. It should be noted for this discussion that Jim demonstrates many of the behaviours of a child with attentional difficulties, including fidgeting, impulsive responding, mental fatigue, distractibility, and some disinhibition. As a result, scores on all assessments should be interpreted with great caution. While the assessments can give a broad picture of Jim's relative strengths and challenges, they cannot be considered to be indicative of his actual ability, which may be significantly greater if his attentional difficulties are accounted for.

Jim's Strengths

Reasoning and Comprehension

Jim scored in the superior range for reasoning ability, particularly when engaged in nonverbal reasoning tasks. Combined with Jim's high scores in existential and visual-spatial intelligence on an inventory of multiple intelligences, it is clear that Jim is a "big picture" learner. This means that Jim will learn best when curriculum is delivered in the context of real life importance and application. The gap between Jim's scores on the verbal and nonverbal portion of the KBIT, while not significant statistically, may have clinical significance. Jim is clearly better able to reason when presented with visual stimuli than when given language input in isolation. Thus multi-modal means of learning and responding will make best use of Jim's gifts and talents.

Multiple Intelligences

Jim has great strengths in existential, visual, interpersonal, and musical intelligences. He loves to learn about the world, is highly spiritual, musical, and visual. Jim has a mature understanding of human social issues and will be motivated by studies that explore deeper issues and applications. For instance, the study of plants will be of more interest to Jim when put in the context of the preservation of the forests for animal habitat, than when focused solely on the parts and functions of a plant.

Reading

Jim's reading, both for decoding and comprehension, scored well above grade level on the Johns BRI. He enjoys reading, and is able to draw information from text in both English and French. However, it should be noted that Jim's difficulties with attention and sequencing may affect his comprehension when presented with longer, more complex passages.

Figure 8.3 cont'd

Portage & Main Press, 2013, *Resource Teachers*, ISBN: 978-1-55379-501-8

Social Cognition

Jim self-reports that he enjoys working with others, prefers group activities to solo ones, and has many friends who seek his company. These are all positive indicators of a strength in social cognition. Given his difficulties with attentional previewing (impulsivity), this is a very significant strength!

Areas of Challenge

Attention

Jim struggles with maintaining his attention and level of alertness. In *All Kinds of Minds* Dr. Mel Levine describes attentional difficulties and challenges as having three main components — processing controls, mental energy controls, and production controls.

Processing controls help students select, prepare, and refine information. Jim struggles with poor saliency determination — he cannot distinguish between important information and details. This affects his learning in several ways. First, he is likely to pay attention to unimportant sensory stimuli, such as sounds outside the room or the feeling of his clothing. This results in high levels of distractibility. Most children are able to screen out such stimuli and, therefore, can concentrate on the important incoming information, like the teacher's voice or the text. For Jim, these filters work only sporadically. Verbal prompts and visual cues (such as "Now this is the important part, so listen carefully") can be of great assistance to children with poor saliency determination. Second, Jim struggles to distinguish the important ideas from details in both his reading and writing. Thus Jim often retells a story rather than giving the main idea when asked, has difficulty determining main events, and often focuses on details in his writing without ensuring a logical flow and sequence to the plot. Graphic organizers that provide a framework for planning will support Jim's thinking in logical ways.

Mental energy controls help students regulate their level of alertness, consistency, and effort. Jim has significant challenges with his mental energy control system. Jim's mind operates like a sprinter or a sports car — fast off the line but poor gas mileage over the long haul. This results in Jim feeling tired, overwhelmed, and anxious which, at times, he interprets as "being bored." Demystification can help Jim significantly with this. Jim now understands his kind of mind and, that when he is facing a "long road trip," he will need to find ways to "gas up" along the way. Taking a quiet stretch break, eating something healthy, self-massage, etc. can all help to refresh his energy level. Teachers can help by chunking tasks into shorter, doable pieces, and allowing Jim to take short breaks. As well, Jim's multiple intelligences profile indicates that he learns well and is stimulated by music and working with others. Listening to an iPod when writing, or working cooperatively with a partner may also help Jim maintain his alertness.

Production controls allow students to control their output, both behaviourally and academically. These controls allow us to think before we act, plan our strategy, and monitor our progress. Jim's "sports car" mind tends to affect his production controls as well. Perhaps because he knows that he tires easily, Jim is anxious to "get things over with" and often rushes through tasks without planning his strategy. When his mental energy begins to wane, he then struggles to monitor his progress, and his level of alertness drops. Explicit use of planning tools such as checklists for task sequence, and graphic organizers, as well as schedules for monitoring time sequences and "gas breaks" will help Jim be more consistent and deliberate in his approach to tasks. The inability to facilitate and inhibit output can

Figure 8.3 cont'd

Portage & Main Press, 2013, *Resource Teachers*, ISBN: 978-1-55379-501-8

also affect motor coordination. Jim demonstrates this tendency in the involuntary sounds and muscle movements present when he attempts to focus on a task. More will be said about this in discussion of Jim's motor skills.

Sequencing and Organization

Jim appears to struggle with temporal sequential ordering. This ability involves being able to interpret, remember, and create information that needs to be in a specific order or sequence. The steps in a mathematical problem, the order of events in a story, the motor movements needed for writing all take the form of sequences. Time is the most important sequence; one has to be able to manage time to successfully complete a task. Knowing what to do first, second, and so on and how long to spend on each step are key skills for task completion. As kids progress in school, the demands for sequential thinking expand greatly. Jim's "big picture" mind has great benefits when approaching an open-ended, creative task. However, when approaching a time-limited structured task, Jim will need assistance to set reasonable plans for approaching the task and completing it on time.

Language Development

Jim scored in the average range for both receptive and expressive vocabulary. Given that Jim is in a French immersion program and therefore spends less time reading and writing in English than the normed population for these tests, his vocabulary is quite acceptable. Jim's reading comprehension is well above grade level, which indicates an ability to comprehend unknown words in context, and draw information at advanced levels. However, Jim's expressive language (i.e., beyond vocabulary) appears disordered sequentially. In other words, while Jim has adequate vocabulary to express his ideas, he is challenged by having to organize his thoughts into a logical sequence and syntax to express his ideas, both verbally and in writing. Jim is aware of this challenge, responding positively to such statements as "A lot of times I have trouble explaining things that I know I understand" and "Sometimes I get mixed up when I have to tell a story." Jim self-reports that responding orally in front of a group or in writing is anxiety-provoking for him as a result.

Motor Output

Jim has an immature pencil grasp and holds his pencil tightly, resulting in early muscle fatigue. He was unable to complete the finger succession task, an indicator of fine motor coordination difficulties. His printing is poor, and his drawings indicate some fragmentation. Jim also reports that he struggles with many gross motor tasks and "falls a lot," tripping even when walking down a hall. An OT assessment is therefore recommended for Jim.

Emotional/Social Development

Jim presents as a bright happy young man. He is social and friendly. However, Jim reports a very high level of anxiety, responding positively on all 7 items of the anxiety scale on the Views Attuned measure, such as "I keep thinking bad things are going to happen to me," "I often worry about the future," and "I'm often afraid I'll get embarrassed in school." Jim appears to be aware that he has some learning challenges, but is afraid to disappoint others or be embarrassed in front of his peers. He reports that he fears being made fun of when others collect his work; so he will need some supports to protect him from shutting down as a result. A counselling referral to assess his level of anxiety and help Jim develop strategies for coping with it would be beneficial.

Figure 8.3 cont'd

Portage & Main Press, 2013, *Resource Teachers*, ISBN: 978-1-55379-501-8

Conclusions

Jim is bright, sociable, and pleasant-mannered. He has significant strengths in reasoning ability, reading, social cognition, existential, visual, and musical intelligences. He faces challenges with attention, sequencing, motor output, and anxiety. With this profile, the following recommendations are made:

Jim is clearly better able to reason when presented with visual stimuli than when given language input in isolation. Thus multi-modal means of learning and responding will make best use of Jim's gifts and talents.

The use of alternative means of responding for students who have challenges with written output can alleviate anxiety, assess their understanding more clearly, and make learning more engaging. Using audio recorders, computers, oral presentations, science-fair-type displays, songs, etc. can allow Jim to show what he knows and be successful.

Verbal prompts (such as "Now this is the important part, so listen carefully") and visual cues (such as a hand signal or a light touch on the shoulder) can be of great assistance to children with poor saliency determination.

Activities that stress relative importance will be key for Jim's development. Working on summarizing, main ideas, etc. will be challenging but important.

Graphic organizers that provide a framework for planning will support Jim's thinking in logical ways by sequencing task order and monitoring for time and progress.

Taking a quiet stretch break, eating something healthy, self-massage, etc. can all help to refresh his energy level. Teachers can help by chunking tasks into shorter, doable pieces and allowing Jim to take short breaks. As well, Jim's multiple intelligences profile indicates that he learns well and is stimulated by music and working with others. Listening to an iPod with classical music when writing, or working cooperatively with a partner may also help Jim maintain his alertness.

At home, insuring that Jim has good sleeping patterns and eats balanced meals frequently during the day will help Jim maintain a more even level of mental energy.

Homework should be kept to a minimum, as Jim's mental energy after a full day of school is unlikely to lead to high productivity in the evenings. Reading and other activities that are within his strengths and, therefore, require less mental energy from him are useful forms of homework, which can teach study skills while not leading to anxiety and frustration.

When doing homework, it is advisable for parents to create a parallel activity (e.g., read alongside, or work at a space nearby) so that there is a minimum of distraction and a model to follow. Jim may also need assistance to get organized and sequence the tasks required of him.

Further assessment should be carried out by an OT for motor difficulties, by a paediatrician for attentional challenges, and by a counsellor for anxiety issues.

Figure 8.3 cont'd

Portage & Main Press, 2013, *Resource Teachers*, ISBN: 978-1-55379-501-8

Debriefing Assessments

1. Share the findings with the student's family, with other teachers, and with the student. You may decide to meet with the student separately, depending on how you think the family will manage.

2. Always begin by repeating the idea that all students have strengths and challenges.

3. Again, demystify the brain and the idea of multiple pathways. Remind parents that students do not choose this behaviour, that they are not lazy or unmotivated.

4. Remind parents that the students are still growing, and the purpose of the assessment is to guide the adults in ways to help and support them. Review the student's strengths and challenges, making clear what you, and they, can do to support the student in both talent development and remediation or adaptation.

5. Talk to the students about what he or she can do to manage, and how you and the team will help.

As the next step, use this student's profile to develop class-wide programming and, if necessary, individualized programming and adaptation for the student. Designing such a program for this student now becomes focused and clear, because you know *why* they are struggling with following instructions and getting their ideas down on paper. You also know how best they learn, and that visuals help them learn. Next, we look at the assessment of behaviour.

Portage & Main Press, 2013, *Resource Teachers*, ISBN: 978-1-55379-501-8

Chapter 9

Functional Behaviour Assessment and Building Behaviour Profiles

Key terms and concepts
- communicative behaviour
- functional behaviour assessment
- setting events
- antecedents
- co-morbid (having two or more existing disorders)

Essential understandings
- Behaviour can be externalizing or internalizing, and both can lead to emotional, social, and learning difficulties for students.
- Students exhibit challenging behaviour as a means, conscious or unconscious, of communicating their needs.
- Assessing a student's behaviour as as expression of needs requires the teacher to recognize that behaviour is triggered by antecedents and reinforced by the consequences. A teacher's response to challenging behaviour may actually reinforce the behaviour.

Behaviour is communication. Every species uses body language and behaviours to communicate — snarls, tail slaps, and tipping over desks all are meant to communicate. There is always motivation and communication behind a behaviour, even if we are not clear what it is. Infants scream and cry for multiple reasons — they may be hungry, ill, or tired, or all three. Like parents, we respond by trying to determine what causes the behaviour. We notice patterns to the behaviour — the time that it usually occurs might indicate hunger or fatigue, the conditions of the environment might be a clue (it could be hot, or cold, or too loud), or our own behaviour might have triggered the crying (e.g., we made a loud noise, put the child in an uncomfortable position, or did not notice something needed). We assume that, as children grow and acquire language, they can communicate their needs in other ways, but it's a false assumption. Some students struggle to express their needs, either because of language or speech difficulties or because of emotional or social inhibitions. Their behaviour communicates, but we are not always listening. The key to behaviour assessment is to step back into the role of detective, and try to determine the motivation and message behind the behaviour.

Portage & Main Press, 2013, *Resource Teachers*, ISBN: 978-1-55379-501-8

Human beings are social animals. The young animals in a pack instinctively seek to please, and respond to, the leaders of the pack. A baby wolf only growls at the alpha male if it believes it is about to be eaten. When a child in a classroom "growls" (i.e., opposes) the alpha leader, it is because they believe they are about to be eaten! We may not know why — perhaps they believe they can't do what is being asked of them, and will look stupid. Perhaps adults in their past have abused their power to hurt them (socially, emotionally, sexually, or physically), and so they do not trust authority figures or those who have power over them. Growling back at a frightened cub is not a professional response. To engage in a power struggle with a student who, for unknown reasons, wants to challenge authority, is not effective — nor is it an educational response. It comes from ego and a need to believe "I am in charge here," which although true is not likely to engage a troubled student in learning and positive relationships. We must determine what the student is really communicating, and find a way to empower the student to make positive choices. That might sound idealistic, but I have seen it work time and time again.

ST-V

Devon

I met Devon in the hallway. Literally. He was always in the hallway, sitting at a desk outside his class, beat boxing and playing with things. Periodically, his teacher would come out, remind him he had work to do or it would be homework, and go back inside. Mr. Smith was a new teacher. He cared about his students and was not a rigid guy. He just didn't know what to do with Devon. He liked him, and Devon liked Mr. Smith. But that didn't matter. Every day, Devon would disrupt the class, get angry when asked to focus on a task, and generally sabotage his relationship with Mr. Smith. Sometimes, the confrontation resulted in threats and swearing, or things being thrown around the room, interruptions for which Devon had been suspended several times.

I taught the same grade as Mr. Smith, and he often asked me for suggestions about dealing with Devon. We knew Devon was significantly delayed in his ability to read, but cognitively, he was bright and capable. Mr. Smith was making adaptations for the reading, and used the Smart Board, the i>clicker (student response system), and other technology to try to engage the students. Nothing stopped Devon's behaviour. It was hard for me to make suggestions without really knowing Devon. I started stepping out into the hallway more, chatting with him, and asking about the tasks he was supposed to be doing to try to get a picture of what was happening for him, but he avoided any academic talk, though he was friendly when chatting socially. It broke my heart watching this bright young man living in the hallway and learning nothing. Total exclusion, socially and academically. So one day in January, I approached Mr. Smith with an idea — which he agreed to immediately.

I gave Devon a passport. I walked up to his desk and handed him a mock passport, with his picture, and asked him if he knew what a passport was. He said yes, you used it for travelling. So I told him he could use this passport for travelling...to my class. Anytime he wanted a break, he was welcome to travel. The look on his face was heartbreaking — pure shock, followed by a cynical "You want me in your classroom? Why?" I told him the truth — I liked him, wanted to get to know him better, hated seeing him in the halls every day, and thought his musical affinity would fit well with the musical rhythmic part of my units (I differentiated all my units, using MI). My hope was that in having him in my class, I could figure out what was happening for him, and then plan interventions, whether he stayed in my class or went back to Mr. Smith's.

I sat down and talked to Devon, explaining how my class worked (kids were in learning teams, cycled through centres based on MI, and so on). He told me he had heard about it from other kids — his best friend Derrick (whom you met in TtD) was in my class. In a very casual tone, I told him I knew verbal-linguistic tasks were not his favourite, and he would have support from his teammates for them, but he had to be fair and, in turn, help his teammates at the musical-rhythmic centre and back them up in the rest. I chose these words deliberately — because they weren't about me, or my expectations, or what he would have to do — there was no power language. Even though they communicated the same thing (what I expected of him), they were put into words he understood — teammates, being fair, and backing each other up.

Devon arrived in the class the next day. My students were surprised, but I told them simply I had invited him to join us, and I set him up with a group and continued on as though there was no issue. And guess what? — there wasn't. At the end of the day, I called Devon aside. I believe in just being honest with kids, so I asked him point blank, "How come you got yourself kicked out every day in Mr. Smith's class, and not here?" He shrugged. I sat down with him and said, "I am really glad you came, and glad it worked for you here. Can you tell me what it is about the way we learn here that worked for you?" He thought carefully about it and said, "I felt like everybody liked me here."

Belonging is critical, and sometimes intangible. Mr. Smith was not a mean guy — but he had not taken the time in September that I had to build community and talk to kids about self-respect and respect for others. We had done the RD program and the kids knew that everyone had strengths and challenges, and everyone had value. Devon didn't know all of this, he just felt it. The group that I set him up with immediately welcomed him, asked him what he was good at, and gave him parts that he could do in what they were working on. It was a safe place — he could face challenges with verbal-linguistic stuff, and use his strengths in musical-rhythmic, and that was cool.

Over the coming weeks I worked with Devon, identifying with him at the end of each day "what worked today," what he was good at, how he learned best, and how he could advocate for that respectfully. Devon worked best hands-on and interpersonally. He could not sit still, or sustain attention, or decode words. We had to overcome his objections to Literature Circles and Writers' Workshop. It was clear that if I ever stepped into power (told him he had to do whatever), it would have blown up, but we were always able to diffuse those moments with non-power-struggle language. He learned to ask if it would be okay to work with a partner, to ask if he could use the manipulatives or the technology, to know that he wasn't stupid. Devon's mother came in three weeks later in tears. She thanked me "for what I was doing," saying her son was a totally different person at home.

Students who have been abused, in one way or another, are just not going to grant you power over them. Devon's mother was a very nice woman. He had a good family. But someone had clearly hurt him, perhaps literally, and perhaps emotionally. The bottom line was this: Devon needed to feel safe, and in control, and that I was nonthreatening.

And then I blew it. We had been working on Devon's reading intensively for a few months, and I celebrated when he read his first chapter book. He became enraged,

Portage & Main Press, 2013, *Resource Teachers*, ISBN: 978-1-55379-501-8

shouting, "You think I'm stupid," swearing and ripping up the book. I tried to talk to him, but it only made it worse. So I backed off, and Derrick and his friends came and talked with him.

For two days, he would not make eye contact with me, and was angry — slamming books and chairs and doors, but he came to the class, and worked with his group, so I let him be. On the third day, I approached him and asked him if we could talk. He didn't say anything, but followed me out of the room. I told him I was really sorry I had hurt him, but honestly didn't know what it was that had made him so upset. His answer? "Do you think I don't know that's a baby book? I'm not stupid."

And then it dawned on me. I was celebrating progress because he had come in not being able to read a pre-primer passage, but was now reading a beginning chapter book. But he was right. The chapter book was a grade 2/3 level, but he wanted to be able to read grade 7 books like the rest of his classmates and he felt patronized by my celebration. I apologized, and told him I understood. I said, "You're right, that was stupid of me. It's not that I think you aren't smart. It's that you have made progress, but of course that's not our end goal. I want you reading at the same level your brain can think, which is much higher than that book." I told him about my own journey, moving from obesity to a healthy lifestyle, and how I hated it when my personal trainer said, "That's great, Jen" for things that were not anywhere near what I wanted to be able to do. I understood his reaction, and I should have known better, and I told him so. He was silent, but nodded and went back to the class. It took weeks before he would work with me again on his reading, but this incident gave me a huge insight.

Mr. Smith and other teachers before him had tried to adapt for Devon, meaning well, but often by simplifying or reducing tasks. This made him feel that they thought he was stupid, and that he would look stupid in front of his peers. This might have been the source of that power issue: Teachers, unwittingly, had been making him feel stupid and, in his mind, humiliating him in front of his peers for years. He was done letting anyone do that.

In the UDL classroom, this didn't happen. Devon was doing what everyone else was doing. There were no adaptations, because the differentiation happened for everybody. At spring break, I gave Devon the choice of remaining in my class or returning to Mr. Smith's class for third term. He chose to return to Mr. Smith's class, saying "I don't want him to feel bad, and I want to see if I can do it now." I spoke to Mr. Smith, helping him to design units for third term that would differentiate for all the class, and maintain high expectations for all of his students. Devon asked me if he could use his passport still, and I reassured him he could. He never did, and I never again saw him in the hallway.

Types of Behaviour

Devon's behaviour was an externalization of his feeling powerless and humiliated. Externalizing behaviours are behaviours that are directed toward others, with a range from verbal opposition and disruption to aggression either verbal, sexual, or physical. Externalizing behaviours express emotions such as sadness, frustration, and anger, but direct them outward. They may also be expressing a need, such as the need to reduce anxiety, interact socially, protect oneself, or get attention or love. Other students internalize, becoming depressed and withdrawn, essentially "shutting down."

Internalizing behaviours are directed toward the self, with a range from depression and withdrawal to substance abuse to self-mutilation and suicide, expressing emotions such as sadness, frustration, and anger, but directing them toward the self. They may also be expressing a need, such as the need to reduce anxiety, feel pleasure (some self-mutilating behaviours release endorphins in the brain), or get attention or love. Internalizing behaviour, in many ways, is far more dangerous. Externalizing behaviour is obvious and results in intervention, but internalizing behaviours can often go unnoticed although they are significant predictors of later pathology. It's important to consider the student who withdraws — or who seems depressed or isolated, or whose behaviour otherwise changes — as being equally worthy of intervention as the student who externalizes.

Neurological Underpinnings of Behaviour

Sometimes behaviour has an underlying neurological or biochemical origin. There are chemicals in our brain that regulate our moods and behaviour. Children who exhibit severe behaviour disorders may have difficulties with:

1. severe, co-morbid attentional disabilities
2. anxiety
3. learning
4. social cognition
5. emotional regulation
6. neurological development

Let's look at these in a little more depth.

1. ADHD: Students with severe ADHD have a reduced inhibition response. Our lower brain is an instinctive brain. Our cortex, or higher brain, acts like the reins on a horse, controlling our instincts and slowing us down so we can think. For instance, when we pick up a hot cup of tea, our instinct is to drop the cup because it's hot. However, our cortex sends the message "Mom's good china!" So instead of dropping the cup, we quickly place it back on the table, and shake our hand from the heat. This message from the cortex to the lower brain is carried by a chemical in the brain called "dopamine." Students who have ADHD have insufficient dopamine or insufficient dopamine receptors, which means that the message is too slow in reaching their instinctive brain. What happens? The student picks up the hot cup, drops it, and 30 seconds later the message arrives: "That's Mom's good china." Now what? This is the student who doesn't — cannot — think before acting. These are the students who start off in early years saying "Sorry" a lot, soon realize that people don't believe them (because it happens too often), and either develop a bravado of "Who cares" or an identity as "the bad kid" because they don't understand why they do

Portage & Main Press, 2013, *Resource Teachers*, ISBN: 978-1-55379-501-8

what they do. They only know they keep getting in trouble. These students cannot think before they act, anymore than a student who has diabetes can regulate their blood sugar voluntarily — both are caused by a lack of a chemical in the body, and are not a choice the student is making, or can make. We must therefore teach students with ADHD how to avoid situations in which impulsivity is likely to get them in trouble, and teach their peers how to support them as they would if they had a group mate who had a visual impairment or physical disability.

2. Students with anxiety disorders may be restless, irritable, tense, or easily tired, and they may have trouble concentrating or sleeping, as do all people when they are feeling anxious. Cortisol in the blood stream prevents concentration and memory, so these students are often mistakenly diagnosed with ADHD or learning disabilities. These students:

    a. are usually eager to please others and may be perfectionists

    b. often have difficulty getting started on a task

    c. need a lot of assurance that they are on the right track

    Reducing pressures for time-limited assignments, making clear the expectations for a given assignment, and frequent conferencing are ways to support these students.

3. Some children with learning disabilities have co-morbid attentional issues. They experience high levels of frustration and anxiety because they are unable to express their thinking or keep up with their peers, and are afraid they will be humiliated if found out. They often, therefore, prefer to be seen as the class clown than as stupid. If presented with a task they do not believe themselves capable of, they will act out in order to be kicked out, rather than have their peers realize they are incapable of the task. Differentiating the instruction and providing opportunities for this student to be successful will reduce such behaviour. They may also seek negative attention because that's what they've grown used to, or they misperceive the expectations because they have difficulties with social cognition.

4. Students with disabilities in social cognition (such as Asperger's) or some students with learning disabilities often:

    a. don't read the reactions of others

    b. don't recognize their impact on others

    c. assume others perceive things the way they do

    d. don't know how to initiate interactions with others in positive ways.

    Frequently, we misread this student as much as they misread us. When the student says, "I was just joking," we don't believe them and instead think they are being manipulative or making excuses. However, if a student cannot read facial expressions and body language accurately, then they may not realize that their behaviour is making another student upset, and

Portage & Main Press, 2013, *Resource Teachers*, ISBN: 978-1-55379-501-8

may persist in doing what they were doing, while truly believing that they are joking.

5. Students with emotional regulation difficulties have difficulty dealing with intense emotion. They may be impulsive, and may not recognize the precursors to their emotional thresholds. If a person doesn't realize he is getting angry, that person cannot take the steps to control the anger (e.g., walking away, asking for clarification of what was said, and so on). Thus they reach a peak of anger without having realized it was developing, and then they explode. Frequently, these students don't have strategies for calming down — it is difficult to take rational steps when one has reached that level of emotional intensity.

6. Seizures, head injuries, brain injuries, and autism can also lead to aggressive behaviour, irritability, and attentional difficulties. Remember, petit mal seizures may not be obvious, or may not even have been diagnosed. Watch for random violence, eye rolling, eyelid fluttering, which can be signs of seizure activity.

Manitoba Policy on Behaviour

For some students, the school division, school or educator will need to approach discipline in a manner that considers the student's exceptional learning needs, including whether:

1. the student was able to access the information

2. the student could understand the policy or rules

3. the disciplinary actions used for the majority of students are appropriate for the student

Appropriate Educational Programming in Manitoba, 2006, p. 18

This policy is critical because it recognizes that students with special needs or neurological disorders may not understand the consequences of their behaviour, or may not be able to control these behaviours. A zero tolerance for violence, for instance, makes no sense when applied to an 8-year-old child with autism who slaps a peer. This does not mean we don't need to intervene. However, expulsion is not an answer. Whether or not students have neurological disorders, behaviour always communicates. Students may be saying:

I don't understand	I want out of here
I'm frustrated	Something is going on for me
I can't do this	I need attention
I'm angry	I'm being abused
I'm scared	I want that!

Portage & Main Press, 2013, *Resource Teachers*, ISBN: 978-1-55379-501-8

Human Needs and Behaviour

Psychology has long explored hierarchies of human need. The most famous hierarchy, posited by Abraham Maslow (1943) detailed five critical needs for human survival: physiological, safety, belongingness and love, esteem, and self-actualization. Maslow believed that people go to extreme lengths to meet these needs, because they experience them as life or death struggles — hence the saying "Dying for love."

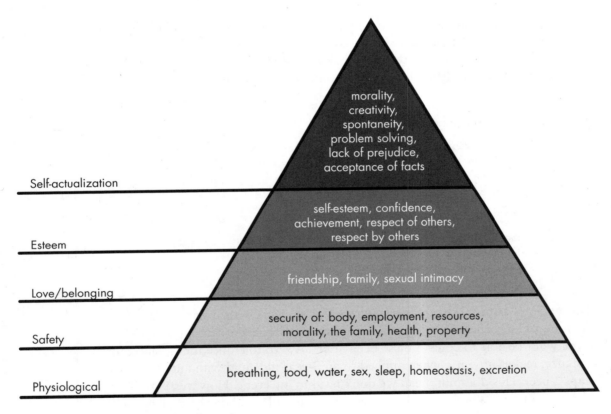

Figure 9.1   Maslow's Hierarchy of Needs

Portage & Main Press, 2013, *Resource Teachers*, ISBN: 978-1-55379-501-8

Hungry children cannot think about learning. Children, too, must first meet their physiological needs — at least for food, water, and sleep — before they can focus on other needs. Figure 9.1 shows the concepts included within all five categories. At the second level of need, physical safety as well as moral safety (i.e., justice and fairness) become the second most important focus for children, though love and belonging include friendships as well as family, esteem, and self-actualization. Since much of learning requires students to be motivated by the last two layers (including self-esteem and achievement, and then learning for learning's sake and personal growth), it is necessary for the first three layers of need to be met first. Devon, for example, was not feeling safe or justly treated and, thus, he was not open to learning.

The nature of Maslow's hierarchy and its cultural bias has been cause for debate. Regardless of whether one believes in the exact order of the types, it's true that all human beings have needs — some physical, some psychological, emotional, and social — that need to be met for them to feel at peace, open to learning, and able to behave in socially appropriate ways.

Tier 1 and Tier 2 Supports

In Tier 1 and Tier 2 of behavioural support, we start, as we do with learning challenges, by conducting ecobehavioural assessment and then by putting strategies in place with the whole class. Try bringing about a change in behaviour by changing what's going on in the classroom, including the sensory environment, the types of tasks being assigned, the length of tasks, and so on. Common strategies used to support students with behavioural challenges include:

a. Chunking: breaking tasks into smaller pieces

b. Organizational supports: visual instructions, colour-coding binders and files, using agendas, materials storage, and so on

c. Flexible groupings: using more small group and partner work, and less whole class and independent seat work to increase engagement

d. Differentiated process: offering multiple process and product choices for students

e. Modelling: showing rather than just telling students what you want, both in learning and in respect for others

f. Cues and prompts

g. Proximity

It's important, especially as we begin to work with an individual student, that we take an approach that is strengths-based. By this, I mean putting the student in places and situations where the problematic behaviour is least likely to occur. We might first avoid placing certain demands on students; for example, we waited a while before implementing a reading intervention with Devon. Such students have

Portage & Main Press, 2013, *Resource Teachers*, ISBN: 978-1-55379-501-8

already spent significant time struggling and failing, which led to their feeling that school is not for them. When we stop expecting them to persevere, and give them a break and a chance to feel successful (to see that they can learn and contribute in school), we will build up their resiliency. We can then have a dialogue with the student about what problems they struggle with, and involve them in planning how we can intervene to support them.

Some students have difficulty discriminating between negative attention and positive attention. All people need attention and, if doing the wrong thing attracts the attention of their teacher and peers, then that is what such students will do. It's important, therefore, to focus on positive reinforcement. Pay attention to what students do well and to when they are doing what you want them to do, rather than focus on them when they are doing something wrong. For example, focus on the class, and give positive feedback to the students who are behaving appropriately — modelling can be a powerful persuader. When Devon was off task and fooling around, I would speak to one of his classmates who was on task, and say something like "Thank you for your leadership and for keeping the group moving forward," and Devon would quickly turn around. Had I said, "Devon, you need to get focused," I would have reinforced in his mind that by being off task he would attract my attention.

Some students have limited ability to sustain attention. No matter how hard they try, they will fail if we expect them to stay on task for extended periods of time. It's simply not possible for them. As a result, we must schedule activities to reflect the students' variable attention spans. For example, it might be more effective to schedule several short sessions rather than one long session to complete a task.

Functional Behaviour Assessment

When a student continues to exhibit challenging behaviour despite UDL interventions, we begin to consider that the student might need Tier 3 supports, such as conducting a functional behaviour assessment (FBA) to determine the cause; that is, what is the student is trying to communicate, and how can we best intervene?

The FBA helps you determine the purpose of the student's behaviour and how you might help replace that behaviour with a more socially acceptable method of achieving the goal. For instance, if the student wants attention or wants to avoid a task, then your request that the educational assistant remove them from the room will only serve to increase the behaviour because you are giving the student what he or she wants — attention and/or avoidance of the task. The next time the student faces such anxiety-provoking tasks, the behaviour will recur and become more frequent, despite the consistent "consequence" of removal from class. We must assess what the student is seeking, in order to avoid accidentally reinforcing the behaviour.

The theory behind FBA is that challenging behaviour most often serves one of four functions:

Portage & Main Press, 2013, *Resource Teachers*, ISBN: 978-1-55379-501-8

1. Avoidance: "I don't want to do this."
2. Escape: "I'm not comfortable here (in this space/setting)."
3. Attention: "I want your and/or my peers' attention."
4. Tangibles: "I want xxxx (sensory stimulation, as in grabbing food)."

Try This

Let's look again at the observations of Jim's behaviour. See pages 50 to 51 in chapter 5.

What do you notice are the patterns of Jim's behaviour? When does he shut down or tune out?

We map out what Jim's current path appears to be. In other words, what triggers Jim's behaviour? What does he do? And what happens when he does it?

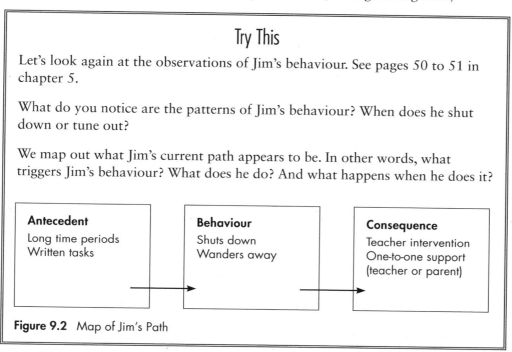

Figure 9.2 Map of Jim's Path

To determine a student's motivations, we must first observe the behaviour in its natural context. When conducting the FBA, we must observe the child over several days and in a variety of contexts (e.g., morning and afternoon, when learning different subjects, with different teachers, in different types of activities, whether group work, hands-on, individual). Note when the behaviour occurs, the context, the level of severity, and the outcomes. Such notes can be categorized on an "ABC" chart, which stands for *antecedent* (what was happening before or as the behaviour occurred), *behaviour* (what the student did), and *consequence* (how people responded and what the adults or peers did) (see pp. 48 to 49).

Conducting a Functional Behaviour Assessment

In this type of assessment, we look for patterns in the behaviour. Does it always happen at a certain time, or when presented with a certain type of task? What consequences are reinforcing the behaviour?

Portage & Main Press, 2013, *Resource Teachers*, ISBN: 978-1-55379-501-8

Analysis of Observations

We can see that Jim's behaviour is attracting attention, and avoidance — of doing the task alone, without support.

Next, we map out the desired pathway. What do we want this student to do instead? For instance, we might want Jim to learn to take a break without distracting others, and then return to work. Or we might want him to learn to ask for options, or for alternative response formats.

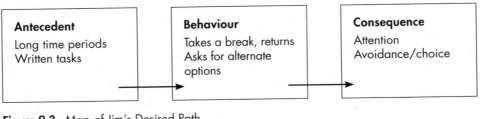

Antecedent	**Behaviour**	**Consequence**
Long time periods Written tasks	Takes a break, returns Asks for alternate options	Attention Avoidance/choice

Figure 9.3 Map of Jim's Desired Path

Now, the programming part is the hard part. We have to stop giving Jim what he wants when he does the wrong thing and, instead, give it to him for doing the right thing. This means we cannot pay attention to him when he shuts down. But we can pull him to the back of the room with the task so he doesn't get to avoid it, and we can tell the EA and his peers to leave him alone. Alternatively, if he does what we want — takes a break, returns, and asks for options, we can reinforce this action with positive attention. If he continues to get attention and avoidance for doing the wrong thing, why would he change? It can be hard to ignore the attention-seeking bad behaviour sometimes, but we must change the pattern. Here, then, is Jim's behaviour plan:

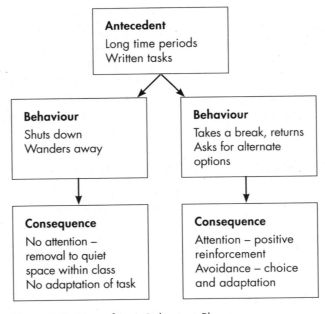

Figure 9.4 Map of Jim's Behaviour Plan

Portage & Main Press, 2013, *Resource Teachers*, ISBN: 978-1-55379-501-8

Of course, to do this, we have to teach Jim how to recognize when he needs a break, what options are acceptable, and how to ask for options respectfully. We can't expect that he will — just magically — do it. However, Jim showed strength in visual learning and social cognition, so we could use visual scripts, or peer coaching and role playing as the means to teach him such a process. Whatever the choice, someone must sit down with Jim and teach this approach. It is important to explain to Jim what you have noticed. You might say to him:

> "I have noticed that it seems difficult for you to stay focused for long periods of time. Your mind seems to be like a race car, brilliant and fast off the line, but runs out of gas quickly. Does it feel like that to you?"

You can then follow up with:

> "Let's talk about how we can handle a race-car mind. If you need to gas up, there are ways to do so that would not disturb your classmates. Do you have any ideas about what would work for you?"

In this way, you give Jim input and you empower him to take ownership of his challenge, and to develop strategies for coping with it. You can't fix his brain, and neither can he. Setting goals in an IEP such as "The student will learn to stay on task for longer periods of time" just sets up for failure any student who has low mental energy.

For a student who is visually impaired, we would never set the goal "I will learn to see," so we should not expect a student with an attention deficit to "pay attention." Because of their disorder, they cannot focus their attention, so we should not punish these children for having an invisible disability. The student with a visual impairment learns Braille, and a student with attention deficit disorder has to learn how to take breaks, to refuel, and to return to work.

You can have a similar conversation with Jim about his challenges with writing, and how you would like him to request supports. Tell him, too, that just shutting down, avoiding, and lying to his mom are only going to result in struggle, whereas if he asks, you can work it out together. Let him know you are on his side. It is possible he feels he would disappoint his mom if she knew he was struggling. Likely, he doesn't want her to see him struggling with his homework — or he just avoids it because it is too hard to concentrate after a full day of school and with family stuff around him. Only when he sees you as an ally will you find out what's happening for him.

Portage & Main Press, 2013, *Resource Teachers*, ISBN: 978-1-55379-501-8

Individualized Programming for Tier 2 and Tier 3 Supports

Chapter 10

From Assessment to Programming a Universally Designed IEP

Key terms and concepts
- individual education plan (IEP)
- goals, strategies, assessment
- talent development
- strengths-based approach

Essential understandings
- An individual education plan (IEP) should outline the goals and strategies for helping the student be successful in their classroom.
- An IEP must be carefully planned to ensure that a student's strengths are developed and that the student has a chance to spend a part of their school day doing what they can do and love to do, not just focus on what they cannot do and on remediation.
- To the greatest extent possible, strategies for supporting learners should be designed using UDL, that is, offered to all students as options so that one student is not singled out.

The whole reason for assessment is to guide programming. Now that we have completed a full learning profile on Jim, we can use his profile to guide our programming and instruction. In Tier 2, we use small-group interventions or individual interventions of short duration, all aimed at success in the classroom. When these are unsuccessful, and we believe a student requires the Tier 3 interventions of individualized programming, we develop a team approach to supporting him by writing up an individual education plan (IEP).

IEP Planning Teams

In departments of education across the country, policies require that classroom teachers, resource teachers, principals, and parents be involved in any IEP planning process. Most provinces, too, include students in the planning. For instance, Prince Edward Island's IEP document states:

> Since individual education planning is all about the student, it follows that the student's presence and involvement is vital to the process. The nature and degree of a student's involvement in the IEP process will vary, but members of the IEP team have a responsibility to ensure that students understand the purpose of their IEP and

Portage & Main Press, 2013, *Resource Teachers*, ISBN: 978-1-55379-501-8

how the goals and expectations in the plan are individually tailored, evaluated, reviewed, and updated. IEP team members must make every effort to encourage students to participate in the IEP.

In a UDL framework, student involvement is critical. We should not decide what is important for any student without consulting the student and their family. Some parents may not realize they have the right to participate. In fact, some RTs or CTs write up IEPs and send them home to parents, asking for a signature. When the signed document is returned, the teacher files it. This practice must change.

Individual Education Plans

In most current IEPs, the first page provides basic information such as the student's name, birth date, any previous test results, and so on. Usually, it also has space for listing the student's strengths and challenges (see simplified example).

Student Information	School Information
Name:	School Name:
Grade:	Classroom Teacher:
Medical Diagnoses (if any):	Resource Teacher:
Previous Assessments:	Other Clinicians / Team Members / Family:
Current Performance in Areas of Strength	Current Performance in Areas of Challenge

Figure 10.1 Basic information for first page of IEP

In most IEPs, however, the subsequent pages focus solely on what the student cannot do, and the goals are oriented toward remediation of the student's challenges. If strengths are acknowledged at all, the goals focus on using the strengths to remediate the weaknesses. Some IEPs can be many pages long, which is overwhelming to students, parents, and often the classroom teacher. It implies that there are "many things wrong with the student that need to be fixed." It is pages and pages of what the student cannot do, with an expectation that by June the student will have made progress in all of these areas. The IEP structure that I suggest is undoubtedly different from what you have seen in schools.

Concise IEPs are much more practical when they are based on detailed assessments that provide a clear picture of the student's strengths and weaknesses and suggest what needs to be done. "SMART" or "measurable" goals are required in the policies of many provinces, for example, New Brunswick's *Educational Planning for Students with Exceptionalities* 2002. As has been typical in education, we have done a bit of a pendulum swing. In the 1990s, IEP goals were often broad and vague. It was difficult to measure progress toward goals such as "interact positively" or "improve reading comprehension." We had no way of measuring whether what we were doing was working, especially in the case of a student with significant disabilities, because small steps toward a goal are the norm for this population, and broad overarching goals take many years to achieve. Without a measure for the smaller gains toward a goal, IEPs can remain unchanged for many years, leaving little accountability for success. The downside of the change to SMART goals is this: they reduce the depth of our curriculum to statistics and ignore the importance of social and emotional learning, which sometimes really cannot be measured.

The IEP that I am suggesting as part of the UDL/RTI model has some similarities to, but more significant differences from, those in current practice. The first page is similar, but the content of the second page differs significantly for the following reasons:

1. Goals in the IEP must focus on using MI and a neurodevelopmental framework. That is, we must set goals related to what is discovered through the assessments about the student's strengths and challenges in such constructs as attention, higher-order cognition, and so on.

2. Most importantly, we must include a section on talent development, setting goals in areas of strength not just in remediation. If we create plans that focus solely on remediation, we ensure that the students spend more time struggling to do remedial work on what they cannot do or do not like and less time working on what they like and are good at. Then we wonder why students disengage from school, have a poor self-concept, and demonstrate challenging behaviours. It is critical that we give students the opportunity to enjoy school and to feel good about themselves within the walls of our classroom communities.

   Too many students who are thought of as dumb at schoolwork go home and take apart television sets or cars and repair them, or they construct intricate models using connecting blocks, or they dance, sing, paint, or look after younger siblings. In other words, they demonstrate high levels of intelligence kinesthetically, visually, musically, and interpersonally. They should be able to see such skills and knowledge valued in their classroom!

3. To the greatest extent possible, strategies for supporting learners should be developed following UDL principles and offered to all students as options so that they don't single out individual students. This means that the strategies we identify in the IEP should be delivered in the classroom to all students, as much as possible. Remember, the goal of the IEP is to help students be successful *in their classroom*!

Portage & Main Press, 2013, *Resource Teachers*, ISBN: 978-1-55379-501-8

Strengthening of Strengths/Talent Development		
Goals/Objectives	**Strategies**	**Assessment Criterion**
1.		
2.		
3.		

Figure 10.2 Sample of second page of a UDL IEP

Let's look at each heading under Strengthening of Strengths/Talent Development

1. **Goals and Objectives**

   a. Goals are set within a student's strengths, focusing purely on the areas in which they can achieve. For example, if a student has strength in musical-rhythmic, then we must look at developing their ability to play instruments, sing/dance, use technology for composing and creating sound effects, and represent musically their understandings of the curriculum (writing raps, creating sound effects for scenes in a novel, and so on).

   b. These goals are what we think the student should be able to do by the end of the school year. The goals should be realistic for that time frame and, whenever possible, should include input from the student: What are their goals for themselves? What skills would they like to develop, or have the opportunity to do or develop? Giving students input into their own goals empowers them and increases their engagement and sense of belonging.

2. **Strategies**

   a. This is what the adults will do to help the student reach their goals. If the student were capable of reaching this goal on their own, they would already have done so. The IEP must document what you will do, as the student's teachers. The student cannot practise what he or she cannot do, which means that strategies such as homework or reading at home will not likely improve the student's fluency or comprehension in reading unless this is an area of strength for them.

Portage & Main Press, 2013, *Resource Teachers*, ISBN: 978-1-55379-501-8

     b. Perhaps the student can independently work toward a goal in his or her areas of strength; for example, a student who has interpersonal strength might set a goal of taking on a leadership role or of developing leadership skills with a strategy such as "Will volunteer as a peer tutor."

3. **Assessment**

     a. The assessment section is not only about evaluating students, it is also about evaluating our instructional support. Have our current procedures and curricular plans worked for this student? If not, we need to try new strategies rather than just marking the goal as "continued" because the student hasn't achieved it.

     b. The assessment section must follow a logical sequence from the goals and strategies. In the above example, if the goal is to develop leadership skills and if strategies include volunteering as a peer tutor and being mentored by the resource teacher, then the assessment must measure how the teacher will know whether, in fact, the student has strengthened their leadership skills. Stating "Will have volunteered" is not enough, because such a statement measures participation, not leadership skills. What are the criteria for leadership? What specifically will you look for in this student? An assessment criterion like "Uses encouraging language when interacting as a peer tutor" or "Brings additional, self-discovered resources to support work as a peer tutor" may be more appropriate. The learning outcomes from specific curricula may also be appropriate.

In the third and final page of the IEP (Figure 10.3), the goals set out must relate to the student's challenges. This page has the same set-up as the page setting out goals for strengthening of strengths. The goals, strategies, and assessment criteria must be outlined so as to monitor both student progress and the effectiveness of our instructional supports.

    UDL does not mean ignoring or pretending there are no challenges for the student. **It means building ramps that allow this student to enter into the learning.** This differs from a remediation approach in that we are not asking the disabled student to practise walking up the stairs. We recognize, instead, that invisible disabilities (such as learning disabilities and attentional deficits) are no more fixable than are visible ones such as paralysis and visual impairments. This does not mean we are giving up on a student. We are not giving up on a visually impaired student when we teach them Braille. Instead, we are finding a way for them to join in the learning and we are honouring their intelligence and capacity for learning. When we teach a student with a learning disability how to use a writing program, or a student with attentional challenges to learn how to take breaks or chunk the steps in completing a task, we are doing the same — we are giving them a way to be successful rather than asking them to do what they cannot do.

Portage & Main Press, 2013, *Resource Teachers*, ISBN: 978-1-55379-501-8

In addition, to the greatest extent possible, we would then teach these strategies to all students in the class because many others will benefit. This approach prevents this student from being pulled out of their classroom for this instruction to take place. In the All Kinds of Minds institute's <www.allkindsofminds.org> framework, they talk extensively about "prevention from humiliation." This means that we do everything possible not to stigmatize students, or make them feel they are "less than" or "incapable." As we discussed in earlier units about ecobehavioural assessment and UDL, by implementing strategies with the entire class, we can avoid this stigma and end up helping students whose disabilities might not be as obvious or severe, but who can also benefit from such instruction. For instance, while a student with ADHD might need to learn how to chunk activities and take movement breaks without disturbing others, there are undoubtedly several other students in the class who could benefit from such opportunities. Similarly, writing programs can be used by all students!

Thus, the final page of the IEP looks like this:

Interventions at the Breakdown Points/ Protection from Humiliation		
Goals/Objectives	Strategies	Assessment Criterion
1.		
2.		
3.		

Figure 10.3 Final page of a UDL IEP

Note that there is room for three goals in each section. While this number is not rigid, I highly recommend that no more than three goals be set in each section, in order not to overwhelm students and teachers. Prioritize and set realistic and achievable goals. Then, replace the goals that have been accomplished with new ones.

Portage & Main Press, 2013, *Resource Teachers*, ISBN: 978-1-55379-501-8

Try This

If you were designing an IEP for Jim, what goals would you set for him to focus on? What strategies would you use to support him?

As you read Jim's IEP, consider these questions: What are the advantages and disadvantages of this format? What impact is it likely to have on students? teachers? schools?

STUDENT INFORMATION

Name: Jim Doe
Grade: 7
Medical Diagnoses (if any): None
Previous Assessments: None

Current Performance in Areas of Strength
(as determined by testing, interviews, and observations)

1. Higher-Order Cognition / Existential Intelligence
   a. Demonstrates analytic and inferential thinking across the curriculum

2. Social Cognition / Interpersonal Intelligence
   a. Works cooperatively, expresses enjoyment of social interactions

3. Spatial Ordering/ Visual-Spatial Intelligence
   a. Strong artistic skills, able to symbolically represent ideas (e.g., draw detailed diagrams)

4. Receptive Language / Reading
   a. Comprehends text and auditory information at an advanced level

5. Musical Intelligence
   a. Performs professionally in boys' choirs, operas

SCHOOL INFORMATION

School Name: Mr. Smith
Classroom Teacher: Ms. Batiste
Resource Teacher: Mr. Intelligent
Other Clinicians / Team Members:

Current Performance in Areas of Challenge
(as determined by testing, interviews, and observations)

1. Attention
   a. Difficulties with saliency determination and distractibility
   b. Mental energy – fatigues quickly, attention span is limited, rushes through work
   c. Production control / impulsivity & task completion – often answers first thing that comes to mind, does not complete tasks

2. Temporal-Sequential Ordering
   a. Expressive language – oral performance lacks logical sequence and flow
   b. Organizational skills – difficulty with steps to a task, materials management, task completion
   c. Time management – forgets due dates, sets unrealistic expectations for assignments/projects given time constraints

3. Neuromotor
   a. Immature pencil grasp, hand fatigues quickly when writing
   b. Gross motor – lacks coordination, strength

4. Emotional development
   a. Reports high anxiety, shuts down in class

Portage & Main Press, 2013, Resource Teachers, ISBN: 978-1-55379-501-8

STRENGTHENING OF STRENGTHS

Goals / Objectives	Strategies	Assessment Criterion
1. Language/Reading: Jim will develop his vocabulary, read advanced level novels, and respond in multiple ways to show his understanding a. Jim will choose novels at an appropriate level of challenge b. Jim will understand and apply the eight SMART reading strategies (higher-order cognition) c. Jim will respond through MI formats to the novels	1. Enrich Jim's reading program to allow him to read advanced-level novels: a. Multi-levelled texts in Literature Circles for whole class b. Introduce SMART reading to class to add a level of depth to Jim's responses c. Assign students to respond in at least three different ways to their novels (e.g., a skit, artistic representation, musical piece)	1. Jim will: a. Read at least three complex novels this year b. Independently use SMART reading and exceed expectations on the performance standards for synthesizing, inferring, imaging, and making connections c. Meet or exceed expectations for reading comprehension through alternative representation formats (e.g., show synthesis through a visual/symbolic representation)
2. Higher-Order Cognition: Jim will further develop his skills in synthesizing and analysis a. Jim will be willing to attempt Type IV problems b. Jim will persevere in attempts to solve the problems	2. Challenge Jim and his classmates with complex questioning, in-depth study: a. Use Bloom's taxonomy to develop higher level questioning b. Present class with Type IV problems to solve in science, math, and social studies — inquiry-based	2. Jim will: a. Respond to high level problems with at least two different possible solutions
3. Social Cognition: Jim will develop his leadership skills in a peer-coaching venue a. Jim will provide support and encouragement to a younger, struggling reader b. Jim will assist in a lunch time music program	3. Provide Jim with the opportunity to read with struggling readers or younger children, and/or to assist in a music program at lunch a. Model supportive language; coach Jim in how to support peers who may be frustrated, struggling b. Encourage Jim to bring in reading/ musical materials he believes his peers might enjoy.	3. Jim will: a. Use encouraging language when interacting as a peer coach b. Bring additional, self-discovered resources to support work as a peer coach

Portage & Main Press, 2013, *Resource Teachers*, ISBN: 978-1-55379-501-8

INTERVENTIONS AT THE BREAKDOWN POINTS/PROTECTION FROM HUMILIATION

Goals / Objectives	Strategies	Assessment Criterion
1. Attention: Jim will develop self-management strategies for his attentional and sequencing difficulties a. Jim will begin to recognize when he needs a break b. Jim will use his agenda, with support c. Jim will complete assignments one step at a time d. Jim will use webs and mind maps to record his ideas	1. Attention: a. Teach Jim and his classmates to recognize when they need a break, and provide socially acceptable options for these breaks (e.g., going for a drink of water, getting a healthy snack and returning quietly to their desk) b. Provide students with an agenda to record homework and due dates, allow for home/school communication – have EA check Jim's agenda at beginning and end of each day c. Chunk materials for amount and duration of work d. Teach students to use graphic organizers to organize their thinking before writing e. Allow partner work, and musical stimulation	Jim will: 1. a. Independently take breaks without disturbing others b. Consistently bring his agenda back and forth from school, and complete homework c. Increase written production and task completion with supports; fully meet criteria for conceptual understanding d. Use at least three different types of graphic organizers independently
2. Neuromotor: Jim will improve his fine and gross motor skills a. Jim will join in one intramural sport b. Jim will improve his keyboarding skills	2. Neuromotor a. OT consult for motor disabilities b. Provide opportunities for Jim to engage in team sports c. Provide technology (iPad or laptop) to aid in written work	2. a. Demonstrate balance abilities and manipulation skills applying mechanical principles for stability, strength, and consistency in cooperative activities b. Demonstrate age-appropriate proficiency in keyboarding, formatting, and use of multimedia presentation formats (e.g., PowerPoint)
3. Social Emotional Learning: Jim will develop techniques for emotional resiliency (i.e., coping with his anxiety) a. Jim will use a breathing exercise to calm down when prompted b. Jim will begin to indicate when he is feeling anxious	3. SEL: a. Family/school to seek counselling for Jim b. Teach Jim calming techniques (e.g., deep breathing, affirmations) c. Hand signal for Jim to use when becoming anxious	3. a. Independently use calming techniques b. Develop greater confidence in his ability to cope, as measured by self-report and decreased use of hand signal

Portage & Main Press, 2013, *Resource Teachers*, ISBN: 978-1-55379-501-8

Analysis of IEP

One advantage to such an IEP is that it gives us a common language (MI and the neurodevelopmental constructs) with which to speak about student learning. Of course, we would have to explain these terms to parents, but they can be put into simple language quite easily, and translated into many languages. For instance, using words like "time management" and "organization" for "temporal sequential" and "thinking," "reasoning," or "problem solving" for higher cognition makes them meaningful for parents. As a short concise document, such an IEP is more likely to actually be used.

Only after we have created an IEP and attempted a team approach to support both the IEP and the student, do we consider whether we should also pursue Level C testing and possible diagnostic procedures. A learning disability is a disability of exclusion; that is, when medical issues have been ruled out, educational opportunities have been provided, and targeted programming has been attempted and is unsuccessful, we then decide that a student who is struggling to learn may have a learning or cognitive disability. We cannot decide this until we have exhausted medical and educational/environmental possibilities for why a student is not learning.

Portage & Main Press, 2013, *Resource Teachers*, ISBN: 978-1-55379-501-8

Chapter 11
Diagnosis and Funding Categories

Key terms and concepts
- learning disability
- ability and achievement gaps
- categorical funding

Essential understandings
- Students who have a learning disability are identified by a gap between their reasoning ability and their achievement.
- Families go through a grieving process when informed their child has a disability, and the stages of grief take time and compassion to resolve.
- Current funding formulas are categorical, and often not in line with inclusive education policy.

When a student continues to struggle to learn, despite a concerted effort, we have to consider the possibility of a disability. We can look at the learning profile we built and reassess the scores we saw, since we now know that they are not due to lack of educational opportunity or environmental support. According to the Learning Disabilities Association of Canada, the minimal definition of a learning disability is "average to above average intelligence (ability), with below level performance (achievement)." This means a student has the ability to reason, think, problem solve, and understand concepts, but is unable to learn a skill (such as decoding or encoding) that they should be able to learn, given their intelligence. Thus, a significant gap between scores is the key to identifying learning disabilities. This can be a gap between ability and achievement or it can be a gap between areas of achievement such as when a student excels in mathematics but struggles to learn to read.

The gap can also be between types of ability, that is, between verbal and nonverbal reasoning or IQ. All students, indeed all people, have strengths and challenges and will have some gap in scores. It's the size and degree of the gap that is telling. For diagnostic purposes, in most provinces a gap of 15 points in standard score, or 1 standard deviation, is considered significant. So, a student with an IQ of 110 and a standard score of 94 for reading would be considered to have a learning disability. A student with an IQ of 110 and a reading score of 102, on the other hand, would not.

Portage & Main Press, 2013, *Resource Teachers*, ISBN: 978-1-55379-501-8

Try This

Look back at Jim's report (page 87). Do any of his scores indicate the possibility of a learning disability?

Spotlight

For a more detailed definition and explanation, visit the LDAC website at <www.ldac-acta.ca/en>.

The thinking behind this is that if a student is intelligent enough to reason and problem solve at age-appropriate levels, that student should be able to read, write, or do math at age–appropriate levels as well. When a student has normal ability and intelligence but is struggling to read, write, or do math, we identify them as having a learning disability because something must be interfering with their learning.

Applying Scores to Assessment of Learning Disabilities

It is possible for a student to be both gifted and learning disabled. A student can have higher-order thinking orally, but struggle with decoding or encoding. Thus students with an IQ of 140 (gifted) but whose reading is at grade level or below would be considered to have a learning disability *even though they are reading at grade level*, because their potential indicates they should be reading *above* grade level and something is interfering with their learning. We have all encountered such students — the ones who in class discussions have great ideas but struggle to write them down or to read the text. They may appear lazy and disinterested because they produce only the minimum required and we assume, based on their oral ability, that they could do more. Sometimes, that's just not the case.

Without gaps, a student is said to be typical because their learning is in keeping with their potential. So for instance, a student with an IQ of 80 (below average) would be expected to be slightly below average in their academic achievement as well. Because there is no gap, they are not considered to have a learning disability. They are achieving the best that they can. Similarly, a student with an IQ of 120 (above average) would be expected to achieve slightly above grade level. Profiles that are even, therefore, are not considered to be a concern unless:

1. IQ below 70 indicates a developmental disability or intellectual impairment
2. IQ above 130 indicates gifted potential (at least, this is the traditional definition of giftedness). More on this in chapter 14.

Portage & Main Press, 2013, *Resource Teachers*, ISBN: 978-1-55379-501-8

Analysis

This is where reasoning comes in. Jim's receptive language (PPVT) had a significant gap from his ability (KBIT). As well, Jim's verbal and nonverbal IQ had a significant gap. However, his being in French Immersion complicates the process of interpreting these scores. We should never diagnose based on Level B assessments anyway; to do so requires a psychologist and Level C testing, but it raises a question as to whether Jim has a language disorder. We also noted that he struggles with attention, which might also affect these scores. Finally, his fine motor skills were in the disabled range. As a result, Jim's profile may merit further investigation if he still struggles after interventions are put into place. Consultations with the psychologist, speech language clinician, and occupational therapist would be in order.

Interpreting Assessments

When clinicians then conduct assessments, they debrief those assessments with the parent, their family, and teachers. They are likely to write up a report similar to what you see in Jim's, although they would not use MI and neurodevelopmental constructs as the framework. Most assessments will include recommendations, which are the keys for classroom teachers. However, be sure that they match what you know about a student's learning profile.

Keep in mind the frustration a student experiences from having a gap. Being an upper-level thinker but unable to show it (with the result of feeling or looking stupid) creates a great deal of frustration and hurt for that student. Challenging behaviour is a likely result until this student is given appropriate programming that lets them feel successful and included. After all, what would your behaviour be like if every day that you came to work, you were made to feel stupid?

Try This

Look at the chart of student scores. What diagnostic category (LD, intellectual disability, gifted) if any, would they fit into? For answers, see page 125.

Grade	Verbal IQ	Nonverbal IQ	Reading	Writing	Math	Diagnosis?
7	110	104	98	105	80	
2	149	140	120	115	118	
11	83	112	80	81	100	
3	64	66	58	71	70	
8	107	99	106	110	98	
5	145	152	140	147	159	

Portage & Main Press, 2013, *Resource Teachers*, ISBN: 978-1-55379-501-8

Diagnosis and Family Acceptance

In chapter 8, we discussed talking to parents about assessments and learning profiles. Talking to parents about students who have learning strengths and challenges is very different from discussing whether a child has a disability. This revelation is a shock to most families, and it takes significant time for them to absorb. Teachers are often frustrated by a family's denial of their child's challenges, but this is a normal reaction to hearing that one's child is struggling or ill. Acceptance of a diagnosis of disability is a grieving process and follows similar stages. Each family proceeds through the stages at their own pace.

Stages:

1. Shock, disbelief, denial
   a. "There's nothing wrong with my child." This reaction can result in blaming the teachers. It's less hurtful and scary to think that your teaching is the problem, not their child.

2. Anger and resentment
   a. "Why my child? Why our family?"
   b. "It must be ___'s fault."
   c. It could be anger at themselves, self-blaming

3. Bargaining
   a. "Well, if we get this treatment, it will fix it, right?"

4. Depression and discouragement
   a. "We've tried everything, there's nothing we can do. No point in participating in school programming."

5. Acceptance
   a. "We can't make it go away, but we can work with it."

This process takes time, and each family will progress through it at their own rate. Cultural values also influence this process — for example, the importance placed on education, the child's place in the family (eldest, middle, youngest), gender roles in their culture, and family or social pressures (fear of being shamed) can all influence this process.

Relationships are everything. Empathy is key, and not taking things personally will save a lot of frustration for teachers. Again, it is natural for parents to want to believe it is something the school is doing rather than a lifelong disability for their child. Parents need to know how to help, and to become empowered, rather than be made to feel helpless. Don't forget that genetics may also play a role — many parents have the same difficulties as their kids. It's not that they don't want to help, they cannot, and are sad that their child has to "go through what I went through."

Portage & Main Press, 2013, *Resource Teachers*, ISBN: 978-1-55379-501-8

Analysis

The answers to the chart on page 123:

1. LD (dyscalculia)
2. Gifted and learning disabled (LD)
3. Learning disabled (LD)
4. Mild intellectual disability
5. No disability
6. Gifted

Debriefing Families about Diagnostic Testing

When discussing the results of diagnostic testing, it is important to avoid making statements that appear to judge the students or their families. Students with disabilities, and their families, should not be led to believe that the student is globally deficient or that they have, in some way, chosen the disability, or that they must be just lazy or unmotivated. Such statements can significantly affect the parent-child relationship. Because the students know that they have been trying their best, the implication that, if they just tried harder, they could do this task leads the child to believe they must be "dumb." Without knowing the specifics of their own learning challenge, they generalize the problem as simply their failure as a person.

The process of debriefing includes demystifying — removing the mystery of the assessment results — for the student and the parents. The teacher or clinician describes and interprets for a student and their parents her or his profile of strengths and weaknesses. It's critical that we emphasize the strengths so that both the parents and the student know what they can be proud of, which helps maintain the parent-child relationship. When we discuss the student's challenges, it's important to be specific so that the student does not think "I'm no good at anything." Demystification should, nevertheless, help create a realistic self-concept for the child; they should leave with the knowledge of what they can be proud of and what they have to offer the world, as well as what challenges they will have to work through if they want to overcome them. The student and their family should leave a debriefing/demystification session feeling hopeful and empowered. For instance, a student with significant challenges in literacy but with strengths in oral comprehension and visual representation can be told they might one day make a great architect or graphic designer, that they should work on their ability to visualize in three dimensions, and that they should consider visualizing what's happening in the story they are reading to support their comprehension.

Funding Based on Diagnostic Labels

The diagnostic label is not very important to us as educators. Having built a profile of the student's learning, we can develop a plan without attaching a label to the student. In some cases, medical labels can guide our programming; that is, knowing one student has ADHD, or is within the autism spectrum, or a has a visual impairment. However, if we have done our job, we already know that the student has difficulty maintaining attention, understanding social situations, or learning visually. As a result, the diagnosis really has two purposes:

1.   Access to supports for the families. A specific diagnosis can help parents gain access to community supports and programs, to financial support for recommended programming, to parent support groups, and to information about parenting and other aspects of their child's disability.

2.   Educational funding. In many provinces, access to funds for educational purposes is tied to specific diagnostic categories, which means that this labelling process is necessary in order to obtain the recommended supports for the child.

Each province has its own funding formula and its own process for accessing the funding. Unfortunately, most formulas and processes are not based on the principles of truly inclusive education. They require the labelling of diagnostic categories that are, by definition, not inclusive and instead single children out. In such cases, resource teachers, clinicians, and even medical personnel face the ethical dilemma of stretching the truth about the child's needs in order to get access to funding. I have had pediatricians ask me, "What do you need?" meaning "What diagnosis do you need in order to get the child support in the school?" Thus, a student on the autism spectrum, for instance, can be diagnosed as having full autism syndrome; and another student's behaviour can be exaggerated for the same reason. The families receive reports or funding applications that paint their child in very negative lights, but have to sign them in order to get their child the help needed despite feeling traumatized and betrayed by the depiction of their beloved child. As well, this process often results in student-specific funding rather than support for inclusive programming.

A better model comes from block funding. If we analyze the amount a school division has spent on support for students with exceptional needs over the last five years, we can determine a trajectory. If this funding were then provided to the divisions and schools without being attached to individuals, schools could flexibly determine whether, in the case of their local context, the money would be best spent on technology for supporting students, co-teachers, educational assistants, multi-levelled texts for core courses, or a mix of the above and other strategies. An IEP for the school could be built that sets out goals for including students with exceptional needs, strategies for achieving those goals, and criteria for assessing success. For example, a school might set the goals of improving the social engagement of learners with exceptional needs and of differentiating instruction for these learners. Their strategies might then include professional development for the teachers and guidance personnel as well as lunchtime monitors for specifically designed social opportunities or activities such as lunch clubs, sign language teachers for all students, resources (e.g., multi-levelled texts, art supplies, software programs) for differentiated activities, co-teachers or specialist teachers, and so on. To monitor progress, they would then need to develop measures of the social inclusion and the degree of differentiation that would be taking place . This not only allows universally designed supports to be put into place, but it also puts the responsibility on the schools and the teachers to focus on it, rather than hire an EA and leave him or her to support the student alone.

Portage & Main Press, 2013, *Resource Teachers*, ISBN: 978-1-55379-501-8

Chapter 12

Including Students with Mild to Moderate Disabilities

Key terms and concepts
- learning disabilities
- attention deficit hyperactivity disorder (ADHD)
- mild to moderate behaviour disorders
- mild to moderate intellectual disabilities
- emotional and behavioural disorders

Essential understandings
- Students with high-incidence disabilities have invisible disabilities, that is, they are not evident physically, but instead are evidenced by learning, emotional, social, and behavioural challenges.
- Students with mild to moderate disabilities can most often have their educational needs met within the inclusive classroom through universally designed instruction and attention to social and emotional needs.
- Remediation programs that are short-term, intensive, and provide the knowledge and skills students need to be successful in their classrooms are not counter to the beliefs of UDL.
- Students with mild to moderate disabilities should not need a modified program. They are capable of learning most or all of the curriculum, with some support.

Students such as Jim, my example of the assessment levels and processes, have mild to moderate disabilities. Teachers in every classroom in this country see such students every year. For most of them, their needs can be met when the teachers use UDL instruction, pay attention to students' social and emotional well-being, and try ecobehavioural assessment to adjust the environment. Such approaches and adjustments reduce the need for individualized programming because intervention is made at the classroom level rather than at the individual level, which assumes quality Tier 1 instruction across the curriculum.

Portage & Main Press, 2013, *Resource Teachers*, ISBN: 978-1-55379-501-8

However, we cannot deny that even the perfect inclusive classroom might have students whose challenges require intensive intervention. A student in grade 7 who is reading at a grade 3 level, for example, might require programming with the goal of helping the student be successful in their own classroom. During the greater part of the day, we support these students by using the framework of the Three-Block Model. The question, then, is how do we integrate remediation into the UDL classroom?

Intensive Skill Interventions

The Three-Block Model of UDL focuses on enhancing inclusive classroom practice, and on providing supports as much as possible within the classroom. However, if a short-term, intensive intervention will provide the knowledge or skill that a student needs to be successful, then teachers should consider intervention programming. For example, a student who has a visual impairment might require pull-out for a short time because he needs to learn Braille and also needs mobility training in order to move independently in their classroom and beyond. After receiving one-to-one instruction in these skills, the student can return to their classroom full time.

There is no simple answer for the student who has significant skill deficits and is reading four levels below his grade. If the student has already received six years of intensive intervention with little gain, then we must accept that we cannot fix this learning disability anymore than we can fix the other student's visual impairment; we can, instead, consider teaching adaptive skills such as using read-aloud software programs. I don't believe that this approach means giving up on the student. We still provide literacy instruction in the classroom, and support the student with some additional instruction during Literature Circles and cross-curricular reading instruction. To suggest that such instruction is not taking place in the student's classroom is fallacious. If that is the case, then the resource teachers should work on supporting the teacher to implement effective programming or they will soon have many more students needing pull-out, a cycle that results in having too many students in Tier 2 and Tier 3 levels of intervention. If the classroom is not working fully with universal programming (Tier 1; see Figure 3.1), do not resort to pull-out programming. Go into the classroom and get it started. All students need ongoing literacy and numeracy instruction.

The issue: Do we continue to remove a student with a disability from the classroom during subjects in which they can, with adaptations, learn and be successful, in an attempt to fix something we cannot fix? What is the cost-benefit of such a practice? In my experience, the emotional cost of ongoing failure and the academic cost of missed instructional time outweigh the benefits of a very slight gain in rote skills. We must look at each case individually. If a student is still young and has not yet received intensive intervention, or if we have acquired a new technique or technology by which daily intensive intervention could result in the student making significant gains, then we should use it with that student. As well,

Portage & Main Press, 2013, *Resource Teachers*, ISBN: 978-1-55379-501-8

a student who has not received individual programming for several years might be ready to benefit from specific instruction.

There is a place in UDL for remediation. However, we must first determine the nature of our beliefs about students and their disabilities. When I ask an English language arts teacher whether a student with a visual impairment can receive an A in their course — even if the novel or play they are studying is not available in Braille, the answer is always yes. When I ask them how they would assess this student, they quickly respond that they would read the text aloud or use an audiobook, and then assess the student's understanding of the book. For the sake of argument then, we are saying that a student who cannot read the text can still receive an A in English. Yet when I ask teachers whether a grade 9 student reading at grade 3 level can receive an A in their course, the answer is almost unanimously no. When asked why, they respond that the student cannot read the texts required in the course, and is not meeting expectations for reading. In other words, a student with a visible disability can be excused from decoding, but a student with an invisible disability cannot, even if they have a documented disability. Why would we punish students with invisible disabilities? Is the act of reading about the physical ability to lift the word off the page? Or is it the ability to appreciate literature, make sense of an author's communication, draw inferences and make connections, analyze plot and character, and so on?

I am not suggesting that we just give the student an A, but I am suggesting that we make the same accommodations for a student with an invisible disability that we would make for a student with a visible one, and then mark them on the depth of their thought, not on the skill of decoding. Similarly, if I ask a teacher whether a student who is quadriplegic and cannot physically write their thoughts on paper can get an A in their course, they almost unanimously reply yes. When asked how they would assess the student, they reply they would ask the student to express their understanding orally, then rate their depth of understanding. Even in English language arts, one can mark an oral presentation for sentence structure, descriptive language, organization, and other mechanics of writing. So it is only the physical ability to put pencil to paper that is compromised, and perhaps their spelling. Many of the students with learning disabilities who struggle with expressing themselves in writing, yet demonstrate a high level of understanding during class discussions, are assessed based on written tests and assignments and receive poor marks, or fail, courses across the curriculum. Again, why would we punish a student for having an invisible disability?

We discussed in earlier chapters how we punish students with invisible disabilities by devising programs on an IEP that requires the student to spend all day doing what they cannot do, and failing. We do not expect a student with a visual impairment to learn to see or a student with a physical disability to learn to walk, but we force students with learning disabilities to spend years in remediation programs that only result in frustration and failure because we refuse to acknowledge that an invisible disability is unfixable. Instead of helping the student see what they can do, and building on their strengths by teaching them how to adapt to their disability as we would do for the student with a visual or physical disability, we focus on what they cannot do and consider that, if we don't keep trying to fix it, we are "giving up."

Such thinking is about our ego, and we must let it go.

Just as a doctor determines the issue by considering the patient's symptoms, reviewing the medical history of what has already been tried, and then researching whether any other treatments might be effective and appropriate, so too must we. It does not make the doctor a bad doctor if she or he determines that all available treatments have already been tried, and they now have to provide health care services and accommodations for their patient. In other words, we must be willing to objectively assess the student's strengths and challenges, look at their past history of instructional opportunity, and determine whether all available treatments or interventions have already been tried. If they have, it does not make us a bad teacher to instead begin to look for accommodations that will provide a quality of life and education for the student.

If there are interventions that you believe have not been tried and are proven to be effective, then by all means offer them to the student. There are many ways to structure such interventions. In one school I worked in, we used a block system. For nine weeks, we pulled students out of class for half an hour a day for intensive interventions in a variety of areas. In the tenth week, we conducted assessments to determine outcomes, and considered which students to return to the classroom, and which students to rotate into the groups. We did not pull any student for more than two rotations a year. We each ran two groups, after which we spent the remainder of our time working in inclusive classrooms or, when necessary, building individual profiles. If one looks at the research and literature for most intervention programs (e.g., Reading Recovery™, Orton Gillingham), this is the recommended practice. In other words, students are supposed to receive intensive intervention for a specified period of time. Being pulled out to resource for a whole year, having resource blocks scheduled in place of electives, and other "life sentences" are definitely not inclusive. Programs such as Reading Recovery™ were never intended to be long-term interventions, nor were they aimed at students more than one or two grade levels below their placement.

Reading Interventions

First and foremost, we must ensure that we have quality literacy instruction in classrooms across the grade levels and the curriculum. No 30-minute intervention can compensate for poor classroom instruction. Far too many students who are struggling with reading do not have disabilities, which is an instructional issue. As I pointed out in chapter 1, we must be willing as a profession to examine what is going well in our field, and what is not. Currently, our reading instruction is producing students who do not meet grade level expectations at a rate greater than 30 percent. Clearly, we need to improve our treatments, and most of this improvement must take place in our classrooms. The overview below reviews the components of reading.

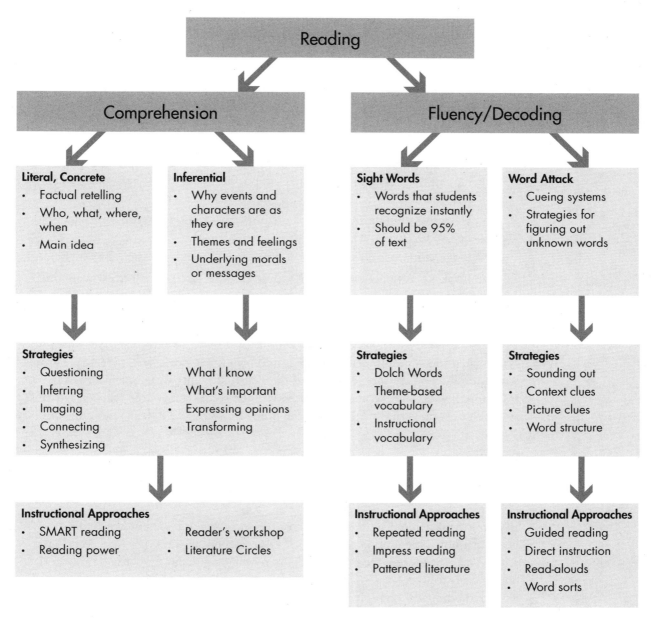

Figure 12.1 Reading deconstructed: Key elements of comprehension and fluency/decoding

Portage & Main Press, 2013, *Resource Teachers*, ISBN: 978-1-55379-501-8

There are two main components to reading: fluency and comprehension. Fluency refers to the ability to recognize the words on the page, while comprehension is the ability to make sense of what you are reading. A good reading program must include instruction in word attack, sight word recognition, literal comprehension, and inferential comprehension in all curricular areas.

For those students who do have reading disabilities, there are literally hundreds of programs available as reading interventions. All are useful for some students and not for others. So how do we decide?

1. First, I am always looking for a program that is not just skills-based. I don't want the student to get a message that reading is just word recognition, writing is just spelling, or numeracy is just computation. I always want an element of thinking!

2. Second, we need to match the program to the student. For this, the key is having built an individual learning profile so we know how this student learns well.

   Does the student have a good memory? If so, a sight word approach may be useful.

   Is the student highly auditory? If so, a phonemic approach may be helpful.

3. Looking at the overview of Reading (Figure 12.1), recall the four main elements of reading: literal comprehension, inferential comprehension; sight words, decoding (word attack) strategies. Which elements does the student struggle with? Which ones are they able to do?

For most students, multi-sensory integrated programs work best, that is, programs that address both comprehension and fluency. If students were able to learn in traditional ways, they would have already done so. As a resource teacher, we must research programs that can address the unique mind of a student with a disability.

One School's Journey and Underlying Beliefs

In one school where I worked as a resource teacher, the issue of non-readers became a hot topic among the staff. Of course, there was no one who could not read at all, but there were many students reading significantly below grade level. So the question was raised about how the resource team could help. A decision was made to institute a school-wide "Drop Everything and Read" time for twenty minutes after recess. During this time, classroom teachers would supervise students in their classroom, including any students with significant disabilities, so that the resource teachers, educational assistants, and administrators were free to work one-to-one with a student for a nine-week period, after which we would rotate

Portage & Main Press, 2013, *Resource Teachers*, ISBN: 978-1-55379-501-8

students. In an attempt to bring elements of specialized reading into a structured program that educational assistants could follow, I created a five-day script that included aspects of several reading interventions I had previously used. It was based on the following beliefs:

1. We must first develop sight words because, if a student has to decode every single word on the page, reading will be incredibly laborious. Repeated readings help to develop sight words. However, asking a student to read the same passage over and over can meet resistance, so it is critical to make a game of it.

2. Second (though concurrent), we need to teach students what to do (i.e., word attack strategies) when they hit a word they do not know. Most students know only one strategy — "Sound it out" — but that is the least efficient strategy for the English language, which is not truly phonemic. Learning to use pictures, context clues, background knowledge, and syntactical and grammatical clues are all critical strategies for decoding.

3. Training students to activate their prior knowledge before reading is important. Many students do not do so, and have no context in mind when they try to decode a text. If, when picking up a book on ancient civilizations, the reader does not think of what they already know, for example, about ancient Egypt, then words like *pyramid*, *sphinx*, and *pharaoh* will be hard to decode.

4. Use neurological research related to the brain and reading. One reading intervention program is the "neurological impress method." Some research has shown that a subgroup of students with learning disabilities activate the visual cortex when reading rather than the language centres of the brain, as most readers do. Impress reading claims to reprogram the brain to use the left hemisphere (i.e., the language centres) rather than the right hemisphere (the visual centres) by reading quietly into the right ear of the student as they read. Reading into the right ear activates the left hemisphere of the brain, because the brain crosses over, that is, the brain processes on the left side what happens on the right side of the body. While I am not convinced that this method works, it certainly is not going to do any harm to sit on the right side of the student when we read with them, so it is worth a try!

5. Students are best able to learn to read the words that are in their oral vocabulary. You can follow up a language experience that involves the student dictating a piece orally or writing it in their own words by then using this passage as material for reading intervention. In this way, the student is more likely to be able to decode and remember the words, as the passage contains vocabulary that is within their own experience. However, if one of the goals is sight word development, having the students

Portage & Main Press, 2013, *Resource Teachers*, ISBN: 978-1-55379-501-8

write their own piece won't work because of the misspellings. Instead, I have students orally dictate a piece and I type it up to use as the reading material.

6.   Multi-sensory is best! Read with the student so that they both see it and hear it. Use tactile materials such as felt and sand as well. Have students use their bodies to imitate the shape of letters. Build words out of Plasticine or other tactile material or use magnetic letters.

7.   For the students who are turned off reading because they don't like sitting still, we need to make reading kinesthetic. Hold up flashcards of verbs and have the student act out the meaning. Have students respond to flashcards of adjectives and some nouns by running or pointing to something in the room that fits the word (e.g., table, book, big, red, delicious, beautiful).

Script for One Week of Tutorials in Reading

This program is designed to be used by educational assistants, but the classroom teacher or resource teacher should monitor it. For younger students, provide a bin of picture books from which students can choose, using a new book each week in the early years. For older students, try printing a page from a website, a text related to a topic of interest, a magazine or newspaper article, or a few pages from a high-interest low-vocabulary novel such as the Orca Young Readers.

Monday

1.   Review words from previous weeks (after the first week).

2.   Student reads passage or book from last week (5 minutes) (after the first week).

3.   Look at the cover of a new book, or diagrams, illustrations, or titles. Predict orally what might happen or what the passage might be about (3–5 minutes).

   a.   For fiction:
   What do you think the story is about? Why do you think so?
   Who might be the main character in the story?
   Where do you think the story takes place?

   b.   For nonfiction:
   What information might this passage contain?
   What vocabulary would you expect to see/hear?

4.   Picture-walk orally with the student (3–5 minutes).

   a.   Page through the book looking at the pictures, diagrams, photographs, noticing what's happening in them (and ignoring the text).

   b.   Review their prediction; any new ideas?

Portage & Main Press, 2013, *Resource Teachers*, ISBN: 978-1-55379-501-8

5. Text-walk (3–5 minutes).

    a. Page through the text, noticing key vocabulary, not yet reading the story, noting anything the student might have trouble reading (1–2 per page).

    b. Discuss the meaning of the words, e.g., "The volcano was erupting." *Ask student if they have ever seen a volcano. Do they know what erupting means?*

6. Have the student record their prediction, either orally or in writing (3 minutes).

Tuesday

1. Review words from previous weeks (5 minutes) (after the first week).

2. Quick review of prediction (2 minutes).

    a. Reread the student's prediction from Monday.

3. Impress reading (5–8 minutes).

    a. Sit on the right side of the student, and read quietly into the right ear.

    b. Have student track (pointing with finger) as you read.

    c. Choral reading, i.e., read together.

4. Student reads to you (10 minutes).

    a. Discuss word attack strategies when student hits an unknown word.

    b. Guide the student to use the Click and Clunk Card, but eventually use independently (see Appendix A.2).

    c. Use the strategy Guess the Covered Word (see Appendix A.1).

5. Language Experience (10 minutes)

    a. Have the student retell the story in sequence in their own words or discuss, telling you what information they learned from the passage.

    b. Scribe their response for them or input it into a word processor/computer to be used for repeat readings on the following days.

Wednesday

1. Review words from previous weeks (5 minutes).

2. Repeated reading (10 minutes).

    a. Using the student's retelling, do several timed trials. Try to improve fluency (time) each trial.

    b. Or, give the student one minute to read aloud as much text as they can; then try to read further each trial.

    c.   Make it a game!

    d.   If the student does not know a word, the teacher tells him or her the word within three seconds.

3.   Literature response (15 minutes).

    Have student write a double entry journal about the story, or act it out, or illustrate a key moment in the story, or create a rap song, or... .

Thursday

1.   Review words from previous weeks (5 minutes).

2.   Repeat reading of passage — one last timed trial. Can you beat your best time? (5 minutes)

3.   Choose 3 key words from the Dolch list that are in the passage. Allow the student to choose 2 or 3 words they want to learn, and do word study, using different strategies each week to see which works best for the student (15 minutes).

    a.   Build with letter tiles, foam letters, and/or similar

    b.   VAKT (visual, auditory, kinesthetic, and tactile — see Appendix A.3)

    c.   Plasticine, and/or similar

    d.   Word work, e.g., if the words are "play," "new," and "good"
        What rhymes with play?
        What rhymes with new?
        What rhymes with good?
        Find other words with similar patterns (e.g., the double o in good)

4.   Write the key words on cards (only the 5 or 6 that you selected), and place them on a key ring for review at the beginning of each period.

Friday

1.   Review words from previous weeks (5 minutes).

2.   Review this week's words (5 minutes).

3.   Use the new words in context; for example, have the student make up a story using them, do a word search in books for them, or any other strategy that reinforces the meanings (8–10 minutes).

4.   Reread original text (10 minutes).

Whether you use this program, another program, or create your own, remember to match the program to the learner, rather than use a favourite program arbitrarily given to all students.

Portage & Main Press, 2013, *Resource Teachers*, ISBN: 978-1-55379-501-8

Writing Interventions

As with reading, writing instruction should take place for most students in the inclusive classroom. We must recognize that writing is an act of communication. It is about sharing our thoughts, feelings, and values with others. There are many ways in which to communicate effectively in writing — there is no one right way to write! We have these structured beliefs about how letters should be formed, what makes an essay — topic sentence, supporting details, and so on. Yet many non-traditional forms of essays have become famous and are considered classic treatises, such as Martin Luther King's "I have a dream" speech. E. E. Cummings became famous as a poet specifically by not following the rules. We must broaden our concept of writing as communication to recognize diversity, creativity, and the flexibility of powerful authorship. Writing is not just printing and spelling, reading is not just sounding out, and numeracy is not just adding and subtracting.

The key issues in writing, then, are:

1. How do we help diverse students see that writing is communication, not just the physical act of putting a pencil on paper?

2. How do we help diverse students understand that writing effectively is a creative and personal act, which nevertheless follows some conventions in order to facilitate communication?

Many writing interventions in elementary schools focus on the physical act of writing. Both printing and cursive writing bring forth many interventions in the early years — a serious mistake because they communicate that it's the physical act of putting pencil to paper is what we mean by "writing." Such instruction should be embedded in context so that students can see that the rote skill is a tool for effective communication, but is not the whole picture of writing. We must also recognize the number of different styles of printing and handwriting in written communications probably equals the number of different dialects and accents in oral communications and presentation. Pulling students out of their classroom to practice a rote skill that could just as easily be embedded in classroom instruction is definitely not UDL. Teaching a student how to use special software or graphic organizers, for example, is an appropriate intervention but most should take place in the classroom and be offered to the whole class. Many students will benefit from learning about possible tools for organizing their ideas.

Numeracy Interventions

As with literacy, we must recognize that there is more to numeracy, more to being a numerate person, than rote skills such as calculating. Many, many students without disabilities do not remember all their math facts either. Of course it is easier to develop numeracy when a student is able to do mental math and, ideally, we want all students to be able to decode, spell, and memorize their math facts. The problem is that the cognitive abilities of memory, sequencing, and spatial ordering underlie these abilities. So students who struggle with these will also struggle with memorizing (and remembering the sequence of) sight words, with spelling, with calculations, and so on. Again, if we accept that such students have an invisible disability that cannot be fixed, we can try several methods of assisting them in their learning but, ultimately, may have to accept that accommodations such as a calculator may be necessary.

Emotional and Behavioural Interventions

We have previously discussed assessment and intervention for students with emotional and behavioural disorders. Developing a safe learning community, student autonomy, and an internal locus of control are critical to the inclusion of students with emotional and behavioural disorders. As with any other intervention, we want to begin in Tier 1 with strategies that are delivered to the whole class (chunking activities, movement breaks, class meetings, and so on). When a student continues to struggle, we conduct assessment to determine the causes of their behaviour. What is not working for them?

Unfortunately, most behaviour intervention programs are based on an old reward-punishment paradigm. In using it, we communicate that we have the power to give or take away things that are important and of value to the student. This is ultimately bound to create more conflict with a student seeking power. Although they may buy in for a short time, thinking their choices are being empowered, they soon recognize that they are being controlled and they rebel. Research tells us that the plans work in the short term but over the long term serve only to increase the challenging behaviour. We must instead seek to empower and to build competency. As we would with a student having any other type of disability, we need to provide this type of student with strategies for adapting to their disability. When a student is struggling with attention, anxiety, depression, or anger, he or she has to acquire the skills to cope with these stresses. To the extent possible, teachers should introduce such interventions with the whole class. After all, who isn't sometimes restless, anxious, sad, or angry? Couldn't all students benefit from learning about strategies for coping when these emotional states?

In the case of some students, as with reading, writing, and numeracy, there may be a short-term intensive intervention that is best delivered with one-on-one instruction. If such an intervention will then allow that student to function within their classroom, then of course it should be done.

Counselling is the one exception to the rule of short-term and intensive intervention. Some students need an ongoing relationship with a trusted adult to help cope with emotional challenges or trauma they have experienced. In this case, long-term intervention is appropriate, and important.

Portage & Main Press, 2013, *Resource Teachers*, ISBN: 978-1-55379-501-8

Conclusion

The vast majority of students with mild to moderate disabilities can be included, without additional interventions, using the Three-Block Model of UDL. These students were the reason for my creation of this model. These students will be in every teacher's class, every year, so it is time that we design our pedagogy to include them and ensure success for them and all our students. At some point in our learning career, we all needed some extra support. Whether because of a learning challenge or an emotional issue, no one spends thirteen years in school without any help, ever. If we improve our Tier 1 instruction, students with mild to moderate disabilities will not need any more support than most students do at some point in their education. They just may need it more often, which would allow us to focus our special education resources on teaching students with significant disabilities.

Portage & Main Press, 2013, *Resource Teachers*, ISBN: 978-1-55379-501-8

Chapter 13
Including Students with Significant Disabilities

Key terms and concepts
- same task, different goal
- access to general curriculum
- valued roles

Essential understandings
- Social inclusion requires that all students play valued roles within a community, and develop a sense of belonging.
- Students who have significant disabilities have typically been viewed through the lens of social inclusion only, with little or no thought to academic inclusion.
- Students come to school to learn. While academic goals may be different, there should be academic goals for all students.

What a person shows of their understanding — and how — is not all that lies within them. Before computers, Stephen Hawking would have been thought to be intellectually impaired. Melinda, too, demonstrated that more lay within her than was apparent to anyone. Acknowledging this new reality is bringing about a profound shift in thinking. Once again, we have to wrestle with our choices:

1. Given that the student currently appears unable to participate actively in the learning (e.g., is nonverbal), do we focus on the knowledge and skills that we believe they need (i.e., life skills)?

2. Do we treat students as though they are cognitively capable, understanding that we have not yet found a way to communicate with them?

Perhaps there is a way to synthesize these two perspectives. One methodology, sometimes referred to as "same task, different goals" can help us to understand.

Modified Programs and UDL

When a student cannot meet age-appropriate learning outcomes, we modify their program. Until recently, this meant giving them a separate program from the rest of the class, resulting in parallel learning (e.g., Sam does science when we do science, but he does a different science). In a UDL program, however, all students continue to learn in interaction with their peers and on the same material as their peers but Sam might be on a modified program. When I say that, I see some people shaking their heads because they are thinking about their Sam and "There's no way Sam can learn what the others can learn." That may be true. However, if the tasks are designed in such a way that they are open to many levels of learning, Sam can engage in the same activity as his peers, even though he may walk away with a different understanding. In any conversation involving multiple people, each individual will walk away with their own understanding of, and perspective on, what was discussed. Students are never all learning the same thing, even if we think we are teaching them all the same thing.

Sam's Story

ST-V

In one high school that I was working with, many of the teachers in the upper grades were struggling to understand how a student with significant disabilities could be reasonably included in their courses. So I asked them in which course they would find it most difficult to include such a student. The answer was grade 12 Pre-Calculus. I asked the teacher what the course was about. At first, he started naming algorithms, but I asked him what the conceptual nature of the course was. He told me it was about mathematical functions and relations — how changing one variable affects another variable. I then asked him: "Who uses Pre-Calculus? Where is it used?" He noted that engineers, predominantly, use the trigonometry and logarithms contained in Pre-Calculus courses. I had done some homework, and learned that surveyors (geographical ones, that is), also used these calculations within their work. So I asked him, "If we gave your students the following project, would they have to use all, or at least most, of the material in your course in order to complete it?"

The project involved putting students into teams of four. Each group represented a construction company, tendering a bid to build an addition to the school. The addition had to have six more classrooms as well as washrooms, and it had to be accessible. The bid required that the company do four things:

1. Survey the schoolyard to determine what land was available, what the limitations were for shape and space considering such things as the need for a football field.

2. Draw a blueprint, to scale, of the proposed addition.

3. Develop the budget they propose for the build, including materials and labour.

4. Create a three-dimensional model (like those that architects use) to show what the addition will look like.

Portage & Main Press, 2013, *Resource Teachers*, ISBN: 978-1-55379-501-8

We involved municipal surveyors, who agreed to come in and show the kids how to use the equipment. The students were taught in stages with brief mini-lessons. For instance, as they moved from the 3-D of surveying to calculating the 2-D blueprint, the teacher gave short mini lessons on algorithms and concepts they would have to consider. The teacher agreed that the project could include most of his curriculum, with some small additions.

The students loved this project. It allowed for hands-on, visual, cooperative learning. The students who excelled in different tasks — building models, drawing, mathematical calculation, oral presentation, and other skills — all had a chance to shine. It was a lot more fun than worksheets of algorithms, and it gave them an applied sense of what Pre-Calculus is about.

And then there was Sam, a student with Down syndrome. He exhibited challenging behaviours when asked to do any academic task, crossing his arms and shouting No. He would flop down on the floor and refuse to get up. At times, Sam would lash out at staff if they got too close when this kind of interaction was happening. However, Sam was also social, and he tried to interact with his peers, smiling and saying Hi. He did not always know how to interact appropriately, but he clearly had the desire to. When I asked Sam's resource teacher about his math, she looked quizzical. They had been trying to teach Sam money and time, without much success. When I asked her if Sam could count, she said, "Yes, to twenty," after which it became somewhat random. Since the unit involved a lot of measurement, I asked her if Sam could use a ruler. She said he had used it as a straightedge, but she doubted that he could use it to measure a specific length. No one had asked him to try take measures, probably since elementary school, if then. Sam's IEP consisted of goals focused on communication (taking turns, making eye contact, increasing vocabulary), following instructions, fine motor skills, and functional life skills, including the mathematics of time and money. I suggested that we set the following additional goals for Sam that are specific to this unit:

Sam will learn his numbers to 30 (which is on a ruler).

Sam will learn to use a ruler both for drawing lines of specific measurements and for measuring lines.

During interactions with his group, Sam would also be able to work on his communication skills, his fine motor skills, and his ability to follow instructions.

I asked the math teacher to select three students from his class that he thought had some leadership and interpersonal skills to work with Sam in a group. We also asked the group to ensure that Sam had a role in the surveying process. We then let them know that when they were creating the blueprint, Sam was to draw the actual blueprint. We wanted his group members to do the calculations, and then instruct Sam. For example, they were to say, "Draw a line of xx cm" then point to an adjoining corner and say, "Now, draw a line of xx cm going this way." We let the students know they might need to show him that he should start at the zero and go to the number of their measure. Finally, when the students were building their model, he was to have a role in the cutting and gluing, thus developing fine motor skills, while chatting and interacting with his peers.

Portage & Main Press, 2013, *Resource Teachers*, ISBN: 978-1-55379-501-8

Sam had an educational assistant, and I asked the EA to stand back from the group and circulate through the class. I told her that the students would be fine showing Sam how to use the equipment and ruler, and that Sam was more likely to take directions and learn vocabulary from his peers than from adults. I asked her to intervene only if Sam became belligerent and if the students were unable to get him to cooperate. We arranged a hand signal between the group and the EA for when they felt they needed her support.

The process was better than we expected, although challenges arose that we hadn't expected — which is typical in inclusive education. Sam did a great job in the surveying. He learned how to hold the pole and read the angle, although he pronounced numbers one at a time (e.g., 45 was "four five"). We also discovered that Sam would follow directions — when she was pretty. At times, he was reluctant to do the paper-and-pencil aspects of drawing the blueprint. However, one of the young women in Sam's group had gone to elementary school with him. Although they hadn't interacted in years, Sam remembered her. Mia, as we'll call her, was able to ask him to do tasks "for me, please, Sam," and he would unwrap his arms and say okay. It didn't hurt that Sam thought she was pretty. She became true friends with Sam, eating lunch and walking around the schoolyard with him. When thanked by Sam's EA for helping him, Mia replied, "I'm not helping Sam. He's my friend, and he is nicer than most guys. We help each other — he's amazing at knowing when something is bothering me." This is true social inclusion, not tolerance or pity for a peer with disabilities — an equal relationship based on mutual respect.

However, this friendship raised a new challenge. Sam had never expressed interest in girls, rather he had always interacted with both genders as his "buddies." Now suddenly, he was experiencing new feelings and, at times, expressing them openly and loudly. Sam, looking at Mia's chest, told her, "You have nice ___." One of the guys in his group promptly smacked Sam on the shoulder and said, "You can't say that to her, Sam. You have to tell us." I asked Mia if she was uncomfortable, to which she replied, "Oh no, he's just saying what all the guys think." New discussions had to be held with Sam's family and workers to determine how to work with Sam about appropriate sexual language and behaviour. I don't consider this a problem. I think it is a victory. Sam had not interacted with his peers as equals on a learning task in years. Now as he began to look at them again, beyond a passing "Hi" in the halls, he was learning typical adolescent behaviours, and facing typical adolescent male emotions and social situations. And they were clearly beginning to see him as one of them or "the guys" wouldn't have said, "Tell us."

In the end, Sam achieved way beyond what was expected of him, and the learning of his peers was not compromised by his presence. Not only did they do all the math they needed to, they also developed leadership skills that will serve them well in the future. In working this way, we can achieve both of the goals mentioned above. That is, we can work on Sam's life skills, such as turn-taking and following directions, and expose him to the general curriculum at its highest levels, realizing that we do not know what he may be capable of learning.

At the end of the term, the math teacher sent an email informing me that several students who had not taken Pre-Calculus 11 were now asking him if they could take Pre-Calculus 12. Word had gotten around that it was "the best course," and he was "the best teacher." He let me know his students had done well on their exams, although he had needed to do a bit of direct teaching at the end of the project about pieces that weren't addressed in it. He felt that the following year he could either alter the project slightly to include them or perhaps develop a second project.

Portage & Main Press, 2013, *Resource Teachers*, ISBN: 978-1-55379-501-8

Sam's story is a Tier 1 intervention — it took place in the classroom, and the design was created to meet the needs of all of the learners. It is an excellent illustration of "same task, different goals." Sam was engaged in the same task, at the same time, with his peers. When they were surveying, so was Sam. He helped create the blueprint, playing a valued role in doing so, and interacted with his peers socially while building the model. However, his goals were different — he was not learning trigonometry and logarithms, he was learning numbers and basic measurement skills. Sam would not get a grade or credit for Pre-Cal, obviously, but he would be assessed against his IEP, and he was highly successful within that plan. The peers in his group learned the same thing as the other students in the class, and Sam's presence did not change their curriculum, or their learning, in any way — except socially. Everyone benefitted, including the teacher, who had less marking, and much more engaged students.

I played the role of the consultant-resource teacher in this scenario. I was not the expert in Pre-Cal, and I did not need to be. I was the design specialist and, between the teacher and me, we were able to create an inclusive Pre-Calculus course! As the unit moved forward, I co-taught in the classroom. You might wonder how, as I did not have the curricular expertise. This is an illustration of collaborative practice. It does not hurt the students to see that teachers don't always know everything. As the kids worked, the teacher and I circulated, supporting their group work and their learning. If the students had a content or skills question, I would frequently respond with "I'm not sure. Let's see if we can figure it out." In other words, I suspended my ego, and modelled persistence through a challenging problem — learning alongside them. If we got totally stuck, we would ask the teacher to come and show us — again, modelling that it is okay to need assistance sometimes. At the same time, when issues arose with Sam, the classroom teacher would attempt to facilitate, then, if needed, would consult with me about ways to support him. That is the beauty of a team. We each felt safe to try and, when necessary, ask for help.

Supporting Academic Inclusion

Our curriculum is a spiral curriculum. Topics repeat with increasing levels of complexity through the years. For instance, let's take a high school science topic like biodiversity. A student with significant cognitive delays might not be able to meet essential understandings at grade level for this topic — or at least appear not to. However, they can learn such concepts as "There are many different kinds of animals and trees," which is an earlier, simpler level of this topic. Some students may be able to learn "Different animals and plants develop different ways of adapting to their environment" (e.g., when looking at colours of fur and what animals eat). In addition, they might have other goals such as "increasing vocabulary, learning social skills, and fine motor development" infused into their curriculum, as Sam did. In this way, students are exposed to the general curriculum, perhaps learning more than we know, and they interact with their peers while simultaneously meeting their IEP goals.

Portage & Main Press, 2013, *Resource Teachers*, ISBN: 978-1-55379-501-8

To be clear, we are not denying that these students require modifications to their program in terms of what they are expected to learn, given our current ability to teach and communicate with them. However, students with significant disabilities can learn alongside their peers in inclusive classrooms. They, too, need to be challenged to learn and grow. The BC Ministry of Education says this well in their special education manual (2011) when they say, "The student with special needs is seen as first a student and not defined exclusively by those special needs." Children with developmental disabilities echo the behaviour and language of those around them. Put them in a room with other children with atypical behaviour, and they become more atypical. Give them appropriate peer models and supports, and they can grow in language and social skills, as described in the Ryndak article (1999) on Melinda.

> Prior to her movement to the inclusive classroom, Melinda's parents had become increasingly concerned about her, and noted that "her behaviour was deteriorating" (p. 7). They thought that behavioural goals should become a priority for her program: "Let's get her acting appropriately and not kicking people, just so she can hold down a job."
>
> Melinda's behaviour changed dramatically when she transitioned to an inclusive classroom. In the segregated classroom, Melinda was consistently off task and refused to do independent seatwork, often yelling, pushing materials away, or physically removing herself. In addition, she frequently spoke loudly and at inappropriate times in the self-contained classroom. However, in the inclusive classroom, few of these behaviours were apparent. Melinda was consistently on task and attempted to do everything her peers without disabilities did. She developed coping behaviours such as learning to say, "Give me a minute" when she felt frustrated or overwhelmed, and modulating her voice tone.
>
> While some of these behaviours may have developed due to maturity, Melinda consistently displayed markedly different behaviour in the self-contained classroom in contrast with when in the inclusive classroom, even during the transition year when she spent part of her day in each setting. It appeared that the modelling of her classmates without disabilities, the increased expectations, and the educational opportunities available in the inclusive classroom affected Melinda's behaviour in positive ways.

For many students with developmental disabilities, it is easier to learn through doing or through visuals than through language. Therefore, when you are working out lessons on the curriculum, consider the vocabulary that the student requires both for oral and sight words, and the amount and pace of language input — that is, your teacher talk or lecture. Using visuals, allowing the students to read at their own pace and at the level they can read, doing hands-on activities, or using technology and films will all support these students. In short, they need to see and experience what you are talking about.

Portage & Main Press, 2013, *Resource Teachers*, ISBN: 978-1-55379-501-8

Cognitive Skills

Many people with developmental disabilities are concrete, visual thinkers. For them, the curriculum has to be logical and sequential, and to build slowly. Teach the concrete and literal first. For example, when discussing feelings, first teach how to recognize feelings, the signs that someone is sad, or mad, or any other mood. Using role-plays to simulate the situation and giving first-hand experience can be an effective tool.

When planning a UDL unit for a classroom that includes a student with a developmental disability, teachers might develop the planning triangle of what all students will know, what most students will know, and what some students will know by the end of the unit. As in the RTI triangle, the bottom row shows what all students, including the student with significant disabilities, should learn. In the middle of the triangle is the description of the "Fully meeting expectations," that is, what most of the students will learn. At the top of the triangle is what some students, the ones who excel in this topic or subject, will know.

Using this device (Figure 13.1), an English teacher at secondary level planned a study of Shakespeare's *Othello*, breaking out the probable knowledge acquisition

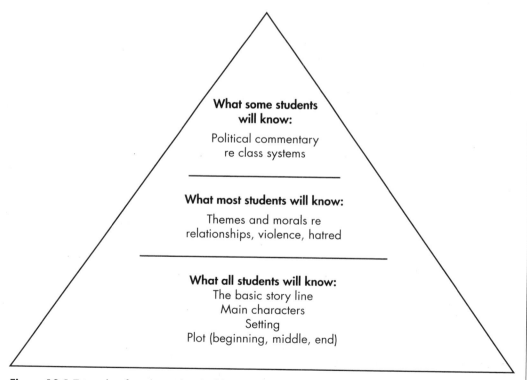

Figure 13.1 Triangle of students' level of learning

Portage & Main Press, 2013, *Resource Teachers*, ISBN: 978-1-55379-501-8

categories. Then the teacher created activities based on multiple intelligences. Students read, acted out, drew, sang, and eventually watched the movie of the play. At the end of the unit, most students wrote an essay as their final project. The student with autism, who was verbal but spoke or wrote only in three- or four-word sentences, was given a story grammar response sheet, and was asked to draw and label his responses. Figure 13.2 shows what he did.

Characters	Setting – Place	Setting - Time
	CYPRUS	LoNg TiMe

Beginning	Middle	End
		LoVe DeAD BAD IDeA

Figure 13.2 Sample of response sheet by student with autism

Did the student get something out of reading Shakespeare? You bet. Was he able to participate alongside his peers, and in so doing, gain social skills, vocabulary, communication skills, and general knowledge? It certainly appears so.

Portage & Main Press, 2013, *Resource Teachers*, ISBN: 978-1-55379-501-8

Self-Help and Life Skills

Traditionally, life skills have been the focus of programs for students with developmental disabilities. The advocates of segregated classrooms for special education argue that the students need to learn life skills such as self-care, mobility, and community living skills more than they need exposure to Shakespeare and other subjects in the general curriculum. The same argument could be made for many students. Many adolescents have no idea how to cook or how to develop a budget, but we don't pull typical adolescents out of math class to teach them how to grocery shop. We act as though students with significant disabilities have no right to determine for themselves what the goals for their education should be, and have no need for an education in an academic sense at all. The *United Nations Convention on the Rights of the Child* discusses both the right to education and the right to education about human rights. Many students now demonstrate the ability to learn much more than we thought they could, and are leading productive lives in the community. However, they cannot do that easily without the ability to read, to write, to express themselves, and to think. Other questions then arise: "Are life skills and academic skills separate or comparable goals? Is it true that students with significant disabilities are best served with a program focused on life skills? If so, do students in segregated classes that focus on life skills develop better skills than those in inclusive classrooms? Is there a way to do both?"

Research shows that students in inclusive classrooms make greater progress in life skills than those in segregated classrooms — even when matched for level of disability and initial level of skills — because of the power of peer modelling. Students with developmental disabilities, even when significantly (or appearing to be) cognitively delayed, echo the students around them. Like a younger sibling, they will imitate their peers and learn by watching and attempting to keep up. Life skills can be combined within the general curriculum. Students in high school who need (or want) to develop the ability to cook meals for themselves and potentially for others as a job placement would need to learn vocabulary such as *mix, stir, boil, melt,* and *pour.* They would also have to learn how to measure ingredients accurately, how to handle hot and cold objects, and how to use sharp utensils safely. Aside from cooking class, where else might these students learn such skills? Chemistry lab, mechanics shop, math class, and other courses all provide opportunities for the development of such skills, while they are also exposed to the general curriculum and interacting with same-age peers. As in Sam's story, the "same task, different goal" pedagogy can be applied. With careful planning, life skills can be developed in an inclusive program from K to 12.

Literacy and Numeracy

For a long time, students with significant disabilities were not taught core curriculum subjects. More recently, programs that seek to teach such students literacy and numeracy skills and concepts have begun to emerge. First, Tier 1 instruction should be implemented as for students with mild to moderate disabilities. Schools should include the students with significant disabilities in classroom-based language arts and math instruction. The teachers should identify goals for them and implement strategies based on the students' strengths. To the extent possible, they should develop UDL interventions and implement them with the whole class, as we did with Sam.

However, if there is a chance that a short-term, intensive intervention could support the student's ability to be successful in their classroom, then it should be provided. I have used two reading programs that proved very successful with this population:

TtD: p. 164

- **Rebus**: This program is as old as the hills, and I don't even know who created it. The idea is to first teach the student to read in pictures, and then help the student to match the pictures to words. This is a "whole word" strategy that uses repetition and visual supports that often work well with students who have significant disabilities. In *Teaching to Diversity* we told the story of José who was taught to read using the Rebus program. Three sets of cards are created (using index size cards with slightly thinner paper so that light can shine through). The first have the pictures only, and the student is taught to associate the picture symbols with the words. The second set of cards has the word and the picture, so the student associates the written word with the picture. The final set of cards has the word on the front, and the picture on the back. Using these cards involves the use of a light box that shines through this set of word cards to reveal images that cue the student as they read. The light box is similar to the old slide viewers — a piece of plastic that the cards sit on with a light bulb underneath. Students read along, and when they get stuck on a word, they turn the light on so that the picture shines through, thus serving as a self-cueing system.

- **Teach Everyone to Read** (TETR): Teach everyone to read is a program designed by Vicki Rothstein and a team of colleagues in the Richmond School Division in BC. This is a brilliant and detailed piece of work in which the stages of literacy from literally "sucking on the book" to emergent reading are delineated. Students are assessed for where they are on the continuum, and goals are set relative to the stages. I used this program with great success for several students with Down syndrome or a disorder on the autism spectrum.

I have not personally used any specialized programs for teaching writing or math to students with significant disabilities. In most cases, the use of multi-sensory approaches such as using manipulatives, or using writing utensils with proprioceptive feedback (sensory feedback to the body's limbs about its position) has been successful within regular classroom instruction — of course at students' own pace for learning.

Portage & Main Press, 2013, *Resource Teachers*, ISBN: 978-1-55379-501-8

Creating Visual Scripts and Social Stories

Many students with significant disabilities struggle to understand social communication — common gestures, facial expressions, tone of voice, and emotional states are all confusing for them. Many tools exist that are frequently used to teach social skills to students with significant disabilities. The UDL approach differs in that we think about the following two aspects:

1. How can we differentiate the instruction so that it is accessible to all students and of interest to most, if not all?

2. How can we present the instruction to all students while not singling out individual students?

Let's look at two commonly used strategies: visual scripts and social stories.

1. **Visual Scripts:** Use a series of pictures or symbols in sequence to show the steps a student must take to complete a task or to manage a behaviour or situation.

2. **Social Stories** were developed by Carol Gray. They were designed as a tool for teaching social skills to children with autism and related disabilities. Social stories provide an individual with accurate information about those situations that he or she might find difficult or confusing. The situation is described in detail with a focus on a few key points:

    ○ important social cues

    ○ events and reactions the individual might expect to occur in the situation

    ○ actions and reactions that might be expected of him/her, and why

The goal of the story is to increase the individual's understanding of the situation in question, make him or her more comfortable, and possibly suggest some responses appropriate to the situation in question. Because some students have difficulty reading social cues and understanding the feelings and perspectives of others, Social Stories attempt to give individuals some perspective on the thoughts, emotions, and behaviours of others. They help the individual better predict the actions and assumptions of their peers. Social Stories also give individuals direct contact with social information through pictures and text instead of through speech or observation. By providing a little distance between teaching and the possible stresses of the social situation itself, they give the student a chance to practise the skills often and on his or her terms.

A Social Story presents this information in four types of sentences:

1. **Descriptive sentences** objectively address the "wh" questions: *where* the situation takes place, *who* is involved, *what* they are doing, and *why* they may be doing it.

2. **Perspective sentences** give readers a peek into the minds of those involved in the story; they provide details about the emotions and thoughts of others.

3. **Directive sentences** suggest desired responses tailored to the individual.

4. **Control sentences** are authored by the student reader as a type of mnemonic device — a sentence to help him either remember the story or deal with a similar situation. These stories are typically used only with fairly high-functioning children.

Spotlight

A program called Boardmaker Studio, which has PicSyms (short for "picture symbols") and templates is available in most schools. You can also find shared scripts and stories using Boardmaker at <www.boardmakershare.com/>.

Sample Social Story: **Sitting on the Carpet**

Sometimes our class sits on the carpet. (descriptive) We sit on the carpet to listen to stories and for group lessons. (descriptive) My friends are trying hard to listen so they can enjoy the story or learn from the lessons. (perspective) It can be hard for them to listen if someone is noisy or not sitting still. (perspective) I will try to sit still and stay quiet during our time on the carpet. (directive)

A good rule of thumb in writing social stories is to write two to five descriptive, perspective, and control sentences for every directive sentence in the story (Gray 1994). Stories should be written in accordance with the student's comprehension skills, and the vocabulary and print size should be individualized for each student. The stories should be written in the first person and in either the present tense (to describe a situation as it occurs) or the future tense (to anticipate an upcoming event). There are two ways to do this in a universally designed way:

1. Make the stories broader in scope so they appeal to same-age peers; role play them and then have students write their own for themselves. This can be like a meditative mantra, where students will have a script or chant in their mind when they are facing a situation that causes them anxiety.

2. Teach social stories as a writing form, and have students write them for a case study or as a service project for students in a nearby elementary class. In this way, all students can be involved in the writing and reading of social stories.

Read the following scenario as an example of a social story. The issue is that the student often screams No at others, including peers, even when they are trying to help. We want to teach the student to say "No, thank you," and be kind and polite to others. However, this student is in grade 8 — not all students need a social story such as the one below, which might otherwise be used for this purpose.

Portage & Main Press, 2013, *Resource Teachers*, ISBN: 978-1-55379-501-8

I am nice to others

When I am at home or at school, I say nice things.
When someone gives me something, I say thank you. If I do not
need something, I say no thank you.
When I speak, I use a quiet voice. I do not yell at others because it
may make them feel bad.
When I am nice to others, I feel happy.

How do we universally design this? We start by having a conversation with all the students about emotions, about how we tend to treat others when we are not happy ourselves. At this level, students can learn about the cycle of behaviour that often permeates conflict: "I feel bad for an unrelated reason, so I snap at you. You feel bad because I have snapped at you, and you reply angrily or storm off. Now I feel even worse because you are mad at me or I have hurt you."

We can talk to students about polite ways to ask for time and space, to say, "No, thank you" when offered help, and suggest how to break the cycle of negativity in relationships by reminding ourselves that we will feel better when we treat others well, even if we are not in a great mood ourselves. In this way, we have broadened the scope of the issue to be applicable to all the students. We can then either teach students about social stories and have them construct one for themselves, or have students write poems or raps or mantras related to this topic. In this activity, then, the student learning this social story will not stand out, as everyone is talking about being kind to others when they themselves are stressed, and developing some kind of repeated affirmation for themselves.

Challenging Behaviour

In chapter 9, we discussed how, when challenging behaviours are present, we conduct a functional behaviour assessment (FBA) to determine the underlying communication. For students with significant disabilities, however, FBA may be more complicated. First, some may be nonverbal so they cannot contribute information as to why they are reacting the way they do. Second, some of their behaviours may be organically driven, at least in part — seizures and other organic disorders can lead to aggression. In my early years as an EA, I worked with Pedro, a student with autism and unrecognized petit mal seizures (we didn't figure that out at first). Pedro was aggressive — hitting, pinching, and biting at what seemed random times. He would be seemingly fine one moment, then suddenly reach over and attack. Other times, his violence seemed goal-oriented or reactive — like when denied access to the fridge or when he wanted something that someone else held. Even looking for his behaviour on our ABC charts, it was difficult to discern a pattern. Then one day, as I was sitting with him, I noticed that he looked at the ceiling just before he became aggressive. I wondered if he was hallucinating or seeing something. He looked almost as if he was watching a movie on the ceiling.

Portage & Main Press, 2013, *Resource Teachers*, ISBN: 978-1-55379-501-8

I approached the psychiatrist in charge, who sent him for neurological assessment. Sure enough, he was having petit mal seizures, dozens of them a day. However, he did not always roll his eyes before becoming aggressive. So we wanted to learn whether the seizures were the cause of his aggression.

When we explored this further, we realized what was happening. As a young child, when Pedro hit or bit, his parents and teachers assumed he was upset or needed something and just couldn't communicate it. Like a crying infant, they responded to him by trying to figure out what he wanted. Was he hungry? Thirsty? Did he have a headache? So while the initial aggression might have been random and organically rooted, Pedro then learned that when he hit, he could get food, a drink, or attention. So now Pedro hit for several reasons — when he had seizures, yes, but also when he was hungry, thirsty, sick, and so on. As a result, when Pedro was medicated for the seizures, his aggression reduced, but did not disappear. We then had to work with him to help him learn other ways of requesting tangibles and seeking attention or care. Teachers should monitor the frequency of such behaviours because they might see a reduction when one variable is altered, but then they may need to look for a second aspect of the behaviour.

Conclusion

Carly Fleischmann is a young woman with autism. She was nonverbal, diagnosed with autism and moderate mental retardation, and had violent and self-abusive behaviours. Carly often stripped off her clothes, spread fecal matter, and displayed other challenging behaviours. Despite this, her parents refused to institutionalize her, and her father would sit and read to her. At the age of eleven, Carly suddenly ran to a computer and began to type. An incredible intelligence and story began to be revealed. Carly now has her own website and blog, in which she talks about life as someone with autism. Imagine how she might be if her father had not read to her. Carly might never have developed a voice, been able to tell her father she loved him, and helped researchers around the world understand the life of someone with autism. She wrote:

> Dear dad, I love that you read to me, and that you believe in me. I know
> I am not the easiest kid in the world. I love you.

All students come to school to learn. It is our responsibility to teach them. All of them.

Chapter 14

Including Students Who Are Gifted

Key terms and concepts
- divergent thinking
- overexcitability
- clustering

Essential understandings
- There are two philosophically different streams in gifted education.
- Some educators define giftedness based on IQ and motivation/achievement.
- Some educators define gifted based on brain research that shows a qualitatively different intellectual and emotional neurology and, therefore, life experience.
- In both cases, asynchrony may be present in gifted children and youth.
- Gifted children are an at-risk population, and one of the least-served populations of students with exceptional needs.

Gifted education has long been a controversial field. Students who are gifted are often under-served in our schools as a result of the myth that, because they are smart, they are lucky and they don't need help. With financial constraints and accountability pressures, many school divisions and even provincial ministries have allowed education for gifted students, to fall by the wayside. Research, however, tells us this is a mistake.

Gifted Education — A Field Divided

When perusing the literature on gifted education, one does not take long to realize that there are fundamental conflicts within the field itself — conflicting definitions of what "gifted" means and conflicting ways of identifying which students are the gifted ones. Unlike such conditions as autism spectrum disorders and learning disabilities, there is no consensus and there is no central body of expertise. Until recently, identification of gifted children relied on one statistic — IQ (intelligence quotient). An IQ over 130 identified you as gifted. If it was 129, too bad for you. Gradually, definitions changed as we realized that one test alone should not be the sole deciding factor. After further exploration, I realized this chaos of opinions fell into two camps, depending on people's motivations:

Portage & Main Press, 2013, *Resource Teachers*, ISBN: 978-1-55379-501-8

Gifted Education as Societal Imperative defined by High Intellect

versus

Gifted Education as Individual Imperative defined as Neurological Syndrome

Historically, gifted education was a societal imperative. In the burgeoning field of cognitive science and subsequently in the "race to the moon," there was an interest in understanding the mind and nurturing "our best and brightest" to move our society forward. When this is the raison d'être of the field, definitions focus on exceptional intellectual ability and performance. Such noted theorists as Joseph Renzulli (2002) and Robert Sternberg (1985) are in this camp, because their definitions require that a student have exceptional ability *and* demonstrate potential or show "task commitment." They have added such criteria as "motivation, task commitment, perseverance" to IQ — but the definition is still focused on intellectual criteria alone.

Sternberg's "triarchic theory of intelligence," for instance, suggests that there are three components to giftedness — analytical, creative, and practical intelligences. More recently, he has discussed "successful intelligence" — which is the ability to achieve success as the individual defines it. Note that, in both cases, the definition requires that a student actively demonstrate these characteristics. There is no room for a student who may have exceptional potential, but does not currently demonstrate that potential. Similarly, Joseph Renzulli's "three ring concept of gifted" includes above average ability, high levels of task commitment, and high levels of creativity. Again, an underachieving student would not be recognized within this model. This makes sense if one's only goal is to provide enrichment to those who might be "the leaders of the future." Students who are not meeting expectations because of social and emotional issues, concomitant learning disabilities, or other environmental factors are not believed to be a good investment for producing a future great scientist or political leader. In a broader sense, if gifted education is seen as being about enrichment or acceleration for those learners for whom the regular curriculum is not sufficient, these models make sense as methods of identifying gifted students, and subsequently programming for them.

However, there is another perspective, brought forward mostly by parents of gifted children, and people in the fields of education and psychological and mental health. This conception of giftedness focuses on the individual's development, and moves beyond the cognitive to include the social, emotional, physical, and sensory aspects of child development. Proponents of this school of thought argue that focusing on performance and achievement external to the child misses out on the key component of giftedness — the internal experience of life as a gifted individual. In this definition, brain research using position emission tomography (PET) scans is cited to recognize that a subgroup of the population differs in brain structure and development, and are thought to be gifted as a result. This neurological research shows that the brains in gifted people have a structure different from that of the average person (O'Boyle 2008). In typical development, the brain undergoes a process of "plasticizing" or "lateralizing" between the approximate ages of 6 and 16. This means the brain develops specialty areas for specific functions. When the technician conducting a PET scan asks the patient to read, the language centres of the patient's brain light up. When the technician asks the patient to walk, the patient's brain involves the motor cortex. In gifted people, the brain does not activate different areas to the same extent. Instead the PET scan shows that multiple areas of the brain in a gifted person become involved in every task — including the limbic system, the emotional centre of the brain. This unique reaction in gifted people is thought to result in global or divergent thinkers who tend to be highly sensitive, anxious, and somewhat perfectionist. Eminent proponents of this definition of giftedness include Dabrowski, whose work is described by M.M. Piechowski and N. Colangelo (1984) and L. K. Silverman (1998) — who are collectively referred to as "the Columbus group."

Kazimierz Dabrowski was a Polish psychiatrist who noted (in his theory of positive disintegration) a group of people who demonstrated five overexcitabilities. These included intellectual, imaginational, emotional, sensual, and psychomotor aspects of their development. *Overexcitability* is a translation, of course, but Dabrowski really meant *a neurological hypersensitivity*. He observed that these individuals have an intense activity of the mind, a vivid imagination, a heightened sensory experience or awareness, a surplus of energy, and heightened emotional sensitivity. Many people working with gifted children today accept this theory, and it is present in the definition put forward by the Columbus group of giftedness:

> Giftedness is 'asynchronous development' in which advanced cognitive abilities and heightened intensity combine to create inner experiences and awareness that are qualitatively different from the norm. This asynchrony increases with higher intellectual capacity. The uniqueness of the gifted renders them particularly vulnerable and requires modifications in parenting, teaching, and counseling in order for them to develop optimally. (Silverman 1998)

Through assessment of the asynchronous development of each of the overexcitabilities (areas of child development), identifying the gifted goes beyond noting the students who demonstrate advanced cognitive abilities. Note that intellectual overexcitability suggests advanced ability and heightened activity, but that might not be demonstrated in or during core curriculum classes. The student who ruminates about life after death, for instance, could be considered to have heightened activity of the mind while not showing "task commitment" in a classroom.

Proponents of this model note that gifted students make up one subgroup (between 2% and 5%) of the population, yet they constitute a much higher percentage of adolescent suicides (Delisle 1986; Dixon and Scheckel 1996). Studies vary as to the rates of categorization or of suicide (as high as 33%), but the rate is disproportional. Identifying gifted children based on IQ and performance offers a simple educational response: we need only enrich their curriculum to meet their needs. Since we are not using social and emotional characteristics to identify them, we are likely to get a homogeneous and relatively well-adjusted population — or they likely would not be performing well.

Portage & Main Press, 2013, *Resource Teachers*, ISBN: 978-1-55379-501-8

However, what of the child or youth who has high potential but is not performing well? What of the child struggling with emotional intensity, high sensitivity, and self-criticism? This is the child who commits suicide, leaving everyone wondering why because they "had everything going for them." About 95 percent of the population has a convergent mind, so our curricula and social world are aimed at a common way of experiencing the world. Being gifted means being an invisible minority, most often not knowing why one doesn't fit in. For a child, and especially an adolescent, this can be interpreted negatively ("I'm weird." "No one understands me." "No one likes me.") and have dire consequences.

Identification and Educational Outcomes

Identifying students using the two different types of definitions results in a different population of students being identified as gifted. Students who are bright, capable thinkers with no evidence of emotional sensitivity, sensory intensity, and so on would be identified as gifted by Sternberg and Renzulli, but not by the Columbus group. In contrast, a student with intense emotionality, higher-order thinking (but not necessarily a high performance level), and a vivid imagination who is struggling to cope in school would be identified by the Columbus group as gifted, but not by Sternberg's triarchic or Renzulli's three ring conception of giftedness.

As a result, the research can be confusing. Some studies suggest gifted students may be at risk emotionally, as noted in the suicide studies. Others say not. Measures of career success, friendships, depression, and so on are similarly discrepant. Of course, this would make sense if one considers that one group might have used an overexcitability measure to identify students, while another might have used IQ and achievement scores. The first would naturally identify a group of students with heightened risk emotionally, and the second would not.

There are criticisms and weaknesses attributed to both definitions. Critics of the cognitive theorists argue that they ignore the emotional and social life of the child and that cultural bias can result from the emphasis on performance. Students learning English as a second language, for example, are unlikely to be identified as gifted because language pervades so many areas of achievement in school. The result of using IQ tests and achievement scores for identification sometimes means that minority groups are underrepresented in gifted programs. By contrast, critics of the Columbus group's definition argue that students who are excelling in curricular studies and activities but do not exhibit any of the social or emotional characteristics might be ignored.

Emerging Conception of Giftedness

Recent research using PET scans has added to the conversation. Using this technology, researchers are able to compare the ways in which the brains of gifted individuals respond as compared to non-gifted individuals. Early results appear to be confirming much of what Dabrowski noted in his clinical observations.

Portage & Main Press, 2013, *Resource Teachers*, ISBN: 978-1-55379-501-8

The brains of people who are gifted respond to some stimuli more quickly, with heightened intensity, and with more areas of the brain involved than do the brains of individuals who are not gifted. This tendency toward divergent thinking — that is, the use of multiple areas of the brain to see connections and the big picture of a task or topic — has benefits and challenges. Divergent thinking does not mean that gifted students are smarter. It means that they think and react differently. Students who are divergent thinkers will be good at open-ended tasks in which the ability to recognize multiple options, grasp abstract concepts, and make connections are valued. In contrast, this kind of mind will find it difficult to undertake a task that requires a logical, sequential follow-through — hence, the stereotype of the absent-minded professor. Organizational skills require convergent, not divergent, thinking.

Perhaps more importantly, when multiple areas of the brain become involved, so too may the limbic systems, the emotional centres. As a result, divergent individuals appear to react emotionally unusually often and unusually intensely to the stimuli that others may not consider a big deal. The sad part of a story, for instance, might start days of rumination for one student when other students have happily gone out for recess 15 minutes later. The resultant social gap can be devastating once other children perceive the divergent child as weird, and the divergent child wonders why they are so different, or why other students don't seem to care.

Thus, we can say that students who are gifted are likely to exhibit high sensitivity in any of the five overexcitabilities, divergent thinking, and emotional intensity, although to varying degrees just as children with autism spectrum disorders vary. Research studies have also noted that perfectionism, anxiety, early language development, and the use of metaphor, rapid speech, sleep disturbance, and other signs of overexcitabilities are often present in students who are gifted. This does not make Sternberg or Renzulli wrong. Individuals who show heightened ability and performance may need enrichment and acceleration to fully optimize their learning and growth. Nor is the Columbus group wrong. Individuals with heightened sensitivity and thought whose experience is qualitatively different from the norm may require specialized supports as well. In universal design for learning, we seek to make the learning community accessible to all students, so we must consider both of these populations in our work.

Tier 1 and the Student Who Is Gifted

At the Tier 1 level, we work as we usually do with any other students. We begin the year by building our classroom community, helping the students get to know themselves and others. Frequently, the gifted students have been overlooked or not identified. At the beginning of the year, therefore, it is crucial for us to be watchful for signs of divergence, of emotional intensity, and of social sensitivity. As we move into regular course content, we monitor these students to ensure that they feel socially and emotionally comfortable, and academically challenged in their areas of strength. In particular, we are watching for:

Portage & Main Press, 2013, *Resource Teachers*, ISBN: 978-1-55379-501-8

1. Social inclusion — Is the student feeling connected, developing a sense of belonging?
2. Emotional health — Is the student resilient, that is, able to persevere through challenges, cope with sensitivity and intensity, and so forth?
3. Engagement in content topics — Is the student engaged in their learning?
4. Divergence/convergence — Given that our curricula, especially in the early years, are convergent, it is important to identify students for whom divergent thinking is dominant, and ensure that these students have opportunities to use their divergent strength, and learn how to complete a convergent process/task.

When a student is obviously having difficulties in any of the above areas, we assess, program, and work together as a team to provide universally designed supports. Many gifted students require specific teaching of organizational skills such as task breakdown, materials management, and time management. When we notice a student struggling with these skills, we can brainstorm with the class to describe the steps to follow in doing the task, and record them on the board. Many students can be helped by learning to chunk activities, to create a timeline, and so on.

Tier 2 and the Student Who Is Gifted

When a student continues to struggle socially, emotionally, or academically in the class, we move to Tier 2, and conduct an ecobehavioural assessment to implement related interventions. As we do with any student, we look for the match between the student and the learning environment. If this student prefers longer work periods that allow time to go in depth (as many gifted students do, because of their intensity and complexity of thought), and if the teacher uses short periods and frequent transitions, the student may struggle because they "are just getting started" when the teacher asks them to put the activity away. Frequently, students who are divergent have many different ideas or possibilities regarding an assigned task (what they will write their essay about, what their main points are, and so on) and will take time or struggle to make a decision before getting started on a task. It would be helpful to provide graphic organizers, to extend time, and to provide opportunities to brainstorm with a partner before beginning.

At this time, we may also begin to build a learning profile. We assess students who might be gifted in the same way as assessing any other student, by creating a profile of their learning strengths and challenges. When analyzing this profile, however, we look closely in literary pieces, methods of solving problems in math, artistic representations, and so on for signs of divergent thinking, high sensitivity, and emotional intensity — both in observed behaviour and in responses to literature, classroom discussions, and so on.

Portage & Main Press, 2013, *Resource Teachers*, ISBN: 978-1-55379-501-8

> ## Try This
>
> Look again at the work samples from Jim in chapter 7, page 71. Do you see evidence of divergence? Of social-emotional intensity?

As we conduct our file review and look at work samples, we look not only for strengths and challenges in neurodevelopmental constructs and multiple intelligences but also for evidence of the three characteristics — other overexcitabilities, exceptional ability, and exceptional performance. Therefore, we might want to consider some unique pieces of a gifted profile. Scales of social and emotional well-being, creativity, overexcitabilities, and problem solving or reasoning ability can be helpful (see Test Instruments, pp. 174–175). Our portfolio might contain:

1. Level A Assessments
   a. Work samples, in domains of strength
   b. Checklists from child, parent, and teacher
      - Multiple Intelligences Survey (see Appendix of *Teaching to Diversity*)
      - Neurodevelopmental Survey
      - Brilliant Behaviours Checklist
      - Developmental characteristics of gifted children
      - SELF Questionnaires
      - Interest inventories
      - Interviews with child, parent, and teacher
   c. Anecdotal observations
2. Level B Assessments
   a. Tests of Ability
      - CCAT
      - KBIT
      - TONI
   b. Tests of Achievement
      - WIAT/PIAT
      - Woodcock-Johnson
      - TOWL
      - KeyMath
      - Reading Assessment
      - PPVT

Of course, we do not conduct all of these. As with other learning profiles, the file review, observations, and analysis of work samples should guide the choice of assessment tools.

Analysis of Jim's Work

When we look at Jim's poem, we can note several things. First, there is a big difference between how he can communicate in print and how he can communicate when using technology. Remember, students who are gifted can also have learning disabilities.

Let's look at the concept of divergence. In this type of thinking, unusual connections are made. For a middle years student, Jim's connection between the imagery of birds and heaven and the idea of a man feeding invisible birds indicate advanced use of imagery, symbolism, and the connection of them. What about emotional sensitivity? What's interesting is that Jim uses little emotional language ("yelled" could perhaps be considered to be emotive). At an age when most students would use direct language to create mood, Jim is able to evoke an image and an interaction that create emotion and power. This kind of subtle sensitivity in combination with imagery, metaphor, and empathy is often an indicator of giftedness.

Analyzing Gifted Portfolios

In statistical terms, researchers have argued whether gifted ability requires 98th percentile and above, or 95th percentile and above. Because we use multiple measures, we consider the Level B and Level A assessments in combination. For instance, a student who is at the 95th percentile in reasoning and has intense emotionality and highly divergent thought might be identified as gifted. In contrast, a student who is at the 95th percentile in reasoning, but shows no evidence of divergence, or social, emotional, sensory reactivity might not be identified as gifted. There is no hard and fast rule. Some school divisions continue to stick with the IQ-based definition of SS=130 (98th percentile) simply because it is easy. However, almost all experts in the field, *from both camps*, agree this is not appropriate, that more than one measure should be used to identify giftedness.

Demystifying Students Who Are Gifted

Students who are gifted may require Tier 2 or Tier 3 supports. They can exhibit internalizing or externalizing behaviours and struggle academically or just disengage as any other student can. In Tier 2, we universally design interventions for gifted students. As discussed earlier, providing supports for convergent skills, opportunities for divergent thinking, and building community and social and emotional well-being, and differentiating instruction can support gifted students. Demystifying students who are gifted and their families can be a delicate task. First of all, many people think that "gifted" equals "smart" and that gifted children are smarter than typical children. Such stereotyping can lead people to place unfair expectations on the child, and create difficulties for sibling relationships. It's best to say that gifted does not mean smarter, and go on to explain the nature of

Try This

Look back at Jim's report on pages 88 to 92. Is there evidence in the scores and test results that could classify him as gifted?

divergent thinking and emotional, social, and sensory sensitivity. Follow this with an overview of the student's strengths and challenges and confirm that the student should not be expected to excel in everything.

Many students do not want to be different in any way. Adults may think being gifted is a gift, but students often see it as meaning they are different when what they want is to fit in. It is important, therefore, to help students understand that all people have strengths and challenges, and that divergence may be a strength of theirs, but they also have others (such as bodily-kinesthetic in athletic activities, or visual-spatial abilities in art) that they share with their peers.

The key to demystification of students who are gifted is the discussion of the overexcitabilities, particularly the emotional intensity. This is the aspect of giftedness that most puts youth at risk — because they feel different, misunderstood, and alienated. Most youth who struggle with depression or attempt suicide indicate that the feeling that "no one understands them" and they "will never fit in" affects them so deeply. It is critical that gifted students and their families understand how their divergent mind leads to more frequent and more intense emotional responses. This knowledge helps the student to accept themselves and not feel that there is something wrong with them for responding the way they do — and at the same time understand why their peers might not respond as they do. An explanation that divergent minds make up between 2 percent and 5 percent of the population allows students to understand that while their experience of the world is in the minority, they are not alone. In a country of more than 30 million people, 5 percent is still at least 1.5 million people — which helps reassure students that they could find people who will understand them and have similar experiences.

UDL and Students Who Are Gifted

The two main curriculum interventions for students who are gifted are acceleration and enrichment. Acceleration is defined as delivering the curriculum at a faster pace (e.g., the student does two grades of math in one year). The negative effects of acceleration on other areas of development, such as socio-emotional, have not been documented, but the risk of doing nothing (not paying attention to clear developmental needs) carries its own risks (Keating 1980). Research studies overwhelmingly support acceleration although many educators resist it as a strategy. Nevertheless, in the majority of documented cases, acceleration has been positive for gifted learners, both those who achieve and those who underachieve. Educators use "enrichment" to encompass several strategies: extending into areas of learning related to the core curriculum, suggesting or using higher level learning

Portage & Main Press, 2013, *Resource Teachers*, ISBN: 978-1-55379-501-8

Analysis

As we look at a completed portfolio, we are looking for strengths and challenges and the presence of the key characteristics of students who are gifted. Many gifted students have domain-specific gifts in that they have exceptional ability in one area only and age-appropriate ability in others. A student can be gifted in math, for example, but have age-appropriate literacy skills. It is also possible to be both gifted and learning disabled. For this reason, we do not expect students who are gifted to excel in everything. We are looking for evidence of exceptional ability in a specific area, and for divergence, emotional and social intensity and sensitivity, and (or) sensory sensitivity. Look at Jim's surveys (see Appendix B). Is there evidence of the three characteristics?

resources and more varied materials, or expanding instructional strategies either within or outside the classroom (Clark 2007).

Teachers who have been implementing universal design for learning can provide both acceleration and enrichment in their classroom. Using MI centres and an inquiry-based approach allows students to proceed at their own pace and to investigate topics and applications beyond that suggested in the regular curriculum. Using Wilhelm's method of inquiry (2007) is another approach. By investigating real problems through professional lenses (e.g., How would a historian view this topic? What would a chemist contribute? What role would each play in the investigation of such topics as sustainability or habitats?), we broaden and enrich students' learning. Such methods as curriculum compacting can be offered to all students; for example, all the students, whether they are gifted or not, who have fully met the expectations for a unit might be offered the opportunity to pursue an inquiry-related topic. The teaching team might develop rubrics that promote higher-order thinking and differentiated tasks so that students will be challenged to learn in multiple ways (e.g., creating a visual representation of cell reproduction).

Meeting the social and emotional needs of students who are gifted is a more complex endeavour. Of course, by beginning with the RD program to help students understand themselves and their peers, to build connections, to use class meetings to resolve issues, and to work in learning teams, a teacher provides support to all students whether or not they are highly gifted in one of the intelligences. The demystification offered through the RD program also is critical and can take place either one-to-one or in groups.

Research also tells us that gifted students benefit both emotionally and intellectually from the opportunity to interact with, and learn from, other gifted students. Students do not need to be gifted in the same domain in order to recognize a peer who is passionate about a topic or the subject as a whole, and who thinks divergently. Such personal connections, which reduce their sense of isolation, can be fostered in two ways — counselling groups and clustering.

Portage & Main Press, 2013, *Resource Teachers*, ISBN: 978-1-55379-501-8

Small group pull-out for counselling helps students who are at risk emotionally. The students in these groups are helped through techniques such as bibliotherapy and videotherapy (featuring characters who are gifted) to feel less isolated and to develop emotional resiliency and coping strategies. This is a Tier 2 or Tier 3 intervention. While the Three-Block Model advocates minimizing pull-out programs as much as possible, in this particular case, social and emotional needs may warrant it.

A preferred method of addressing the need for connection among students who are gifted is clustering. Clustering involves placing a small group of gifted students together in a heterogeneous, inclusive classroom. Conditions should include:

- a classroom teacher with background, or at least interest, in gifted education
- flexible grouping and programming options within the class

Clustering students serves a dual purpose. By placing a small group of students who are gifted together in an inclusive classroom, we allow ourselves to flexibly group the students (i.e., sometimes together, and sometimes spread into different groups), thus facilitating the option of providing enrichment projects and accelerated material. Perhaps more importantly, clustering allows students who are gifted to see that they are not alone in their way of experiencing the world. It reduces alienation and loneliness while at the same time providing students with the chance to learn how to work with diverse others — and isn't that what UDL is all about?

Conclusion

Inclusive education is what will lead to an inclusive society. In our schools, every student, family member, community member, and staff member must be valued for who they are and what they contribute to the community. Children who grow up in such an environment will know themselves as worthy, and recognize diverse others for the richness they bring to our world.

Portage & Main Press, 2013, *Resource Teachers*, ISBN: 978-1-55379-501-8

The Three-Block Model of UDL started out as survival. Survival for a young teacher — me — in very diverse classrooms, trying to meet the needs of my students. It evolved with study, research, experience, and a great deal of collegial input — from incredible master teachers all the way to brand new student teachers — into a framework for inclusive education now being implemented by schools from Kindergarten through grade 12 in six different provinces from coast to coast.

It is more than survival now. It is also more than theory or framework, model or strategy.

It is a vision, an imagination, a belief system. Not in the exact pieces or steps or even blocks — they will continue to evolve and grow, but in the hearts of those in classrooms across this country who are working to make it come to life, to make inclusion come to life.

It is a vision of a truly inclusive educational system.

It is the imagination to flexibly implement it in such wide-ranging settings as remote First Nations community schools, urban inner-city high schools, and private preparatory academies.

It is a belief that it can be done.

Portage & Main Press, 2013, *Resource Teachers*, ISBN: 978-1-55379-501-8

References

Austin, Vance L. 2001. "Teachers' beliefs about co-teaching." *Remedial and Special Education* 22 (4): 245–255.

Bennett, Sheila. 2009. "Including students with exceptionalities." Research Monograph 16, in series *What Works? Research into Practice*: Toronto, ON: Ministry of Education, Literacy and Numeracy Secretariat, and Ontario Association of Deans of Education.

Brackenreed, Darlene. 2011. "Inclusive education: Identifying teachers' strategies for coping with perceived stressors in inclusive classrooms." *Canadian Journal of Educational Administration and Policy* 122: 1–36.

Bru, Edvin. 2009. "Academic outcomes in school classes with markedly disruptive pupils." *Social Psychology of Education: An International Journal* 12 (4): 461–479.

Burgstahler, Sheryl, and Chuan Chang. 2009. "Promising interventions for promoting STEM fields to students who have disabilities." *Review of Disability Studies: An International Journal* 5 (2): 29–47. See <www.washington.edu> for further information on Dr. Burgstahler and her work.

Carroll, Diane, Connie Fulmer, Donna Sobel, Dorothy Garrison-Wade, Lorenso Aragon, and Lisa Coval. 2011. "School culture for students with significant support needs: Belonging is not enough." *International Journal of Special Education* 26 (2): 120–127. <www.internationaljournalofspecialeducation.com>.

Clark, Barbara. 2007. *Growing up gifted: Developing the potential of children at home and at school,* 7th ed. New Jersey: Prentice-Hall, A Pearson Education Company.

Cole, Cassandra M., Nancy Waldron, and Massoumeh Majd, and Susan Hasazi. 2004. "Academic progress of students across inclusive and traditional settings." *Mental Retardation: A Journal of Practices, Policy and Perspective* 42: 136–144.

Crisman, Belinda W. 2008. "Inclusive programming for students with autism." *Principal* 88: 28–32.

Curcic, Svjetlana. 2009. "Inclusion in PK–12: An international perspective." *International Journal of Inclusive Education* 13 (5): 517–538.

Delisle, James. 1986. "Death with honors: Suicide among gifted adolescents." *Journal of Counseling & Development* 64 (9): 558–60.

Dixon, David N., and Jill R. Scheckel. 1996. "Gifted adolescent suicide: The empirical base." *Journal of Secondary Gifted Education* 7 (3): 386–392.

Giangreco, Michael F. 2010. "Utilization of teacher assistants in inclusive schools: Is it the kind of help that helping is all about?" *European Journal of Special Needs Education* 25 (4): 341–345.

Giangreco, Michael F., and Mary Beth Doyle. 2002. "Students with disabilities and paraprofessional supports: Benefits, balance, and band-aids." *Focus on Exceptional Children* 34 (7): 1–12.

Glass, Theresa. 2013. "Creating learning environments for disengaged boys: Bridging the gender gap with universal design for learning." (master's thesis, University of Manitoba)

Gray, Carol. 1994. *Social stories*. See <www.amazon.com/The-New-Social-Story-Book/dp/1885477201/ref=sr_sp-atf_title_1_2?ie=UTF8&qid=1377055897&sr=8-2&keywords=carol+gray+1994>. See also <www.thegraycenter.org/social-stories/carol-gray>.

Jackson, P. Susan. 1998. "Bright star–Black sky: A phenomenological study." *Roeper Review* 20 (3): 215–221.

Jimenez, Terese Carmen, Victoria L. Graf, and Ernest Rose. 2007. "Gaining access to general education: The promise of universal design for learning." *Issues in Teacher Education* 16 (2): 41–54.

Kalambouka, Afroditi, Peter Farrell, Alan Dyson, and Ian Kaplan. 2007. "The impact of placing pupils with special educational needs in mainstream schools on the achievement of their peers." *Educational Research* 49: 365382.

Katz, Jennifer, and Pat Mirenda. 2002a. "Including students with developmental disabilities in general education classrooms: Educational benefits." *International Journal of Special Education* 17: 14–24. Retrieved from <www.internationaljournalofspecialeducation.com/>.

_____. 2002b. "Including students with developmental disabilities in general education classrooms: Social benefits." *International Journal of Special Education* 17: 25–35. Retrieved from <www.internationaljournalofspecialeducation.com/>.

Katz, Jennifer, Pat Mirenda, and Stan Auerbach. 2002. "Instructional strategies and educational outcomes for students with developmental disabilities in inclusive multiple intelligences and typical inclusive classrooms." *Research and Practice for Persons with Severe Disabilities* 27 (4): 227–238. Retrieved from <www.ingentaconnect.com/content/tash/rpsd/2002/00000027/00000004/art00001>.

Katz, Jennifer, and Marion Porath. 2011. "Teaching to diversity: Creating compassionate learning communities for diverse elementary school communities." *International Journal of Special Education* 26 (2): 1–13.

Katz, Jennifer, Marion Porath, Charles Bendu, and Brent Epp. 2012. "Diverse voices: Middle years students' insights into life in inclusive classrooms." *Exceptionality Education International* 22 (1): 2–16.

Katz, Jennifer. 2012a. *Teaching to diversity: The three-block model of universal design for learning*. Winnipeg, MB: Portage & Main Press.

_____. 2012b. "Reimagining inclusion." Canadian Association of Principals. *CAP Journal*. Summer 2012: 22–26.

_____. 2012c. "Making imagination real: Inclusive education and the three-block model of universal design for learning." Canadian Association of Principals. *CAP Journal*. Summer 2012: 30–34.

Katz, Jennifer, and Brent Epp. 2013. "Leadership and inclusion: Leading inclusive schools and the Three-Block Model of UDL." Canadian Association of Principals. *CAP Journal.* Winter 2013: 8–11.

Katz, Jennifer. (in submission). "Implementing the three-block model of universal design for learning (UDL): Effects on teachers' self-efficacy, stress, and job satisfaction in inclusive classrooms K–12." *Canadian Journal of Education* 36 (1): 153–194.

Keating, Daniel P. 1980. "Four faces of creativity: Continuing plight of the intellectually underserved." *Gifted Child Quarterly* 24 (2): 56–61.

King-Sears, Margaret. 2009. "Universal design for learning: Technology and pedagogy." *Learning Disabilities Quarterly* 32: 199–201.

Kortering, Larry J., Terry W. McLannon, and Patricia M. Braziel. 2008. "Universal design for learning: A look at what algebra and biology students with and without high incidence conditions are saying." *Remedial and Special Education* 29 (6): 352–363. doi: 10.1177/0741932507314020.

Koster, Marloes, Han Nakken, Sip Jan Pijl, and Else van Houten. 2009. "Being part of the peer group: A literature study focusing on the social dimension of inclusion in education." *International Journal of Inclusive Education* 13 (2): 117–140.

Kurth, Jennifer, and Ann M. Mastergeorge. 2010. "Individual education plan goals and services for adolescents with autism: Impact of age and educational setting." *Journal of Special Education* 44 (3): 146–160.

Levine, Melvin D. 2002. *Educational care: A system for understanding and helping children with learning problems at home and in school,* 2nd ed. Cambridge, MA: Educators Publishing Service.

Lipton, Laura, and Bruce Wellman, with Carrlette Humbard. 2001. *Mentoring matters: A practical guide to learningfocused relationships,* 2nd ed. Arlington, MA: MiraVia.

Little, Mary E., and Lisa A. Dieker. 2009. "Co-teaching: Challenges and solutions for administrators." *Principal Leadership* 9 (8): 42–46.

Mace, Ronald L., Molly F. Story, and James L. Mueller. 1998. "A brief history of universal design." In T*he universal design file: Designing for people of all ages and abilities.* Raleigh, NC: Center for Universal Design. North Carolina State University. <www.design.ncsu.edu/cud/publications/udfiletoc.html>.

Maslow, Abraham. 1943."A theory of human motivation." *Psychological Review* 50: 370–396.

Mastropieri, Margo A. 2001. "Is the glass half full or half empty?: Challenges encountered by first-year special education teachers." *Journal of Special Education* 35 (2): 66–74.

McLeskey, James M., Michael S. Rosenberg, and David L. Westling. 2010. *Inclusion: Highly effective practices for all students.* Pearson Higher Education. See <www.pearsonhighered.com/product?ISBN=0136101321#sthash.rSunV9Xm.dpuf>.

McNeely, Clea A., James M. Nonnemaker, and Robert W. Blum. 2002. "Promoting school connectedness: Evidence from the national longitudinal study of adolescent health." Journal of School Health 72 (4): 138–146.

Meo, Grace. 2012. "Curriculum planning for all learners: Applying universal design for learning (UDL) to a high school reading comprehension program." *Preventing School Failure: Alternative Education for Children and Youth* 52 (2): 21–30. <dx.doi. org/10.3200/PSFL.52.2.21-30>.

Myklebust, Jon Olav. 2006. "Class placement and competence attainment among students with special educational needs." *British Journal of Special Education* 33 (2): 76–81.

O'Boyle, Michael. 2008. "Mathematically gifted children: Developmental brain characteristics and their prognosis for well-being." *Roeper Review* 30 (3): 181–86.

Piechowski, M. M., and N. Colangelo. 1984. "Developmental potential of the gifted." *Gifted Child Quarterly* 28: 80–88.

Renzulli, Joseph S. 2002. "Emerging conceptions of giftedness: Building a bridge to the new century." *Exceptionality* 10 (2): 67–75.

Rose, David H., and Anne Meyer. 2002. *Teaching every student in the Digital Age: Universal Design for Learning.* Alexandria, VA: ASCD.

Ryndak, Diane Lea, A. P. Morrison, and L. Sommerstein. 1999. "Literacy before and after inclusion in general education settings: A case study." *Journal of the Association for Persons with Severe Handicaps* 24: 5–22.

Silverman, Linda Kreger. 1998. "Through the lens of giftedness." *Roeper Review* 20 (3): 204–210.

Sternberg, Robert J., ed. 1985. *Beyond I.Q.: A triarchic theory of intelligence.* Cambridge: Cambridge University Press.

Stoeger, Heidran, and Albert Ziegler. 2010. "Do pupils with differing cognitive abilities benefit similarly from a self-regulated learning training program?" *Gifted Education International* 26 (1): 110–123.

Symes, Wendy, and Neil Humphrey. 2010. "Peer-group indicators of social inclusion among pupils with autistic spectrum disorders (ASD) in mainstream secondary schools: A comparative study." *School Psychology International* 31 (5): 478–94.

Talmor, Rachel, Sunit Reiter, and Neomi Feigin. 2005. "Factors relating to regular education teacher burnout in inclusive education." *European Journal of Special Needs Education* 20 (2): 215–229. doi:10.1080/08856250500055735

Timmons, Vianne, and Maryam Wagner. 2008. "Inclusive education knowledge exchange initiative: An analysis of the Statistics Canada Participation and Activity Limitation Survey." Canadian Council on Learning website: <www.cclcca.ca/CCL/Research/Funde dResearch/201009TimmonsInclusiveEducation.html>.

UNESCO. 1994. *Salamanca Statement and Framework for Action on Special Needs Education from the World Conference on Special Needs Education: Access and Quality.* Salamanca, Spain, 7–10 June 1994. Paris: UNESCO.

Wilhelm, Jeffrey. 2007. *Engaging readers and writers with inquiry.* New York: Scholastic.

Portage & Main Press, 2013, *Resource Teachers*, ISBN: 978-1-55379-501-8

Provincial Documents

Alberta Learning. 2004. *Standards for special education.* <education.alberta.ca/media/511387/specialed_stds2004.pdf>.

British Columbia Ministry of Education. 2011. *Special education manual.*

Manitoba Education, Citizenship and Youth. 2006. *Bill 13: Appropriate educational programming in Manitoba: Standards for student services.* <www.edu.gov.mb.ca/k12/specedu/aep/pdf/Standards_for_Student_Services.pdf>.

New Brunswick Department of Education. 2009. *Definition of inclusion*, p. 3.

New Brunswick Department of Education. 2002. *Guidelines and standards: Educational planning for students with exceptionalities*, p. 9. <www.gnb.ca/0000/publications/ss/sep.pdf>.

Newfoundland and Labrador Department of Education. 2011. *Service delivery model for students with exceptionalities.* Professional learning package, p. 8. <www.cdli.ca/resources/sdm/DocumentSection/SDM.pdf>.

Nova Scotia Education Student Services. 2008. Fact sheet: "Inclusion: Supporting all students" to support its *Special education policy.*

Ontario Ministry of Education. 2005. *Education for all: The report of the expert panel on literacy and numeracy instruction for students with special education needs, kindergarten to grade 6.* p. 11. <www.edu.gov.on.ca/eng/document/reports/speced/panel/speced.pdf>.

Ontario Ministry of Education. 1998. *Individual education plan (IEP). Resource guide.* <www.edu.gov.on.ca/eng/general/elemsec/speced/iepeng.pdf>.

PEI Department of Education, Student Services. 2005. *Individualized educational planning (IEP): Standards and guidelines. A handbook for educators.* <www.gov.pe.ca/photos/original/ed_ieplanning.pdf>.

Quebec Ministry of Education, Recreation and Sports. 2004. *Individualized education plans: Helping students achieve success. Reference framework for the establishment of individual education plans.* <www.mels.gouv.qc.ca/sections/publications/publications/EPEPS/Formation_jeunes/Adaptation_scolaire/GuideUtili_CanevasPlanInterv_a_1.pdf>.

Portage & Main Press, 2013, *Resource Teachers*, ISBN: 978-1-55379-501-8

Test Instruments

Tests of Ability	Tests of Achievement
Brilliant Behaviours Checklist Author: Kanevsky, Lannie. 1997. *Brilliant Behaviours Checklist: Characteristics of Gifted Individuals*. Burnaby, BC: Simon Fraser U. Level A	**Clinical Evaluation of Language Fundamentals**, 5th ed. (CELF–5) Authors: Eleanor Semel, Elisabeth H. Wiig, Wayne A. Secord Level B <www.pearsonassessments.com/>
Bruininks-Oseretsky Test of Motor Proficiency, 2nd ed. (BOT–2) Level B <www.pearsonassessments.com/>	**Johns Basic Reading Inventory** (BRI), 11th ed. Authors: Jerry L Johns, Laurie Elish-Piper <www.kendallhunt.com/default.aspx>
Canadian Cognitive Abilities Test (CCAT) Level B <www.assess.nelson.com/group/ccat-k.html>	**KeyMath** 3™ Diagnostic Assessment Level B <www.pearsonassessments.com/keymath.aspx>
Concentration Cockpit, Examiner's Guide Dr. Mel Levine Level A <exceptionalresources.pbworks.com/f/Concentration%20Cockpit.pdf>; and <www.allkindsofminds.org/>	**Kaufman Test of Educational Achievement**, 2nd ed. (KTEA–2) Authors: Alan S. Kaufman, Nadeen L. Kaufman Level B <www.pearsonassessments.com/>
Conners 3™ (ADHD assessments) Author: C. Keith Conners Neurocognitive <www.pearsonassessments.com/>	**(Marsh) Self-Description Questionnaire** III Authors: Herbert W. Marsh, Rosalie O'Neill Level B <www.uws.edu.au/cppe/research/instruments> <www.education.ox.ac.uk/research/self/resources/>
Expressive Vocabulary Test, 2nd ed. (EVT–2) Author: Kathleen T. Williams Level B <psychcorp.pearsonassessments.com/HAIWEB/Cultures/en-us/Productdetail.htm?Pid=PAa30750>	
Facial Expression of Emotion: Stimuli and Tests (FEEST) Authors: A. Young, D. Perrett, A. Calder, R. Sprengelmeyer, P. Ekman Level B <pearsonassessmentsupport.com/support/index.php?View=entry&EntryID=825>	**Peabody Individual Achievement Test (PIAT)** Level B <www.pearsonassessments.com/>
Kaufman Brief Intelligence Test, 2nd ed. (KBIT–2) Authors: Alan S. Kaufman, Nadeen L. Kaufman Level B <www.pearsonassessments.com/>	**Social Skills Improvement System** (SSIS) Frank Gresham, Stephen Elliott Level B <www.pearsonassessments.com/>
Learning Potential Assessment Device (LPAD) Reuven Feuerstein <www.scel.org/services/assessment.asp>	**Test of Pragmatic Language**, 2nd ed. (TOPL–2) Level B <www.mayer-johnson.ca/>
Minnesota Multiphasic Personality Inventory® (MMPI–2™) Authors: Ekman, Friesen, Lutzker, 1962 <www.pearsonassessments.com/>	**Test of Written Language,** 4th ed. (TOWL–4) Authors: Donald D. Hammill, Stephen C. Larsen Level B <www.pearsonassessments.com/>

Portage & Main Press, 2013, *Resource Teachers*, ISBN: 978-1-55379-501-8

Tests of Ability	Tests of Achievement
Naglieri Nonverbal Ability Test, 2nd ed. (NNAT®–2) Authors: Jack A. Naglieri Level B <www.pearsonassessments.com/>	**Wechsler Individual Achievement Test** (WIAT®–III) Level B <www.pearsonassessments.com/>
Peabody Picture Vocabulary Test (PPVT™–4) Authors: Lloyd M. Dunn, Douglas M. Dunn Level B <www.pearsonassessments.com/>	**Woodcock-Johnson Tests of Achievement** Level B <www.assess.nelson.com/test-ind/wj-3-ach.html>
Stanford-Binet Intelligence Scales, 5th ed. (SB–5) Level C <www.riverpub.com/products/sb5/>	
Test of Nonverbal Intelligence, 4th ed. (TONI–4) Authors: Linda Brown, Rita J. Sherbenou, Susan K. Johnsen Level B <www.pearsonassessments.com/>	
Wechsler Intelligence Scale for Children, 4th ed. (WISC®–IV) Level C <www.pearsonassessments.com/>	
Wechsler Physical Symptom Inventory (WPSI) Level C <www.pearsonassessments.com/>	
Woodcock-Johnson Tests of Cognitive Abilities, 3rd ed. (WJ–III) Authors: Richard Woodcock, Mary E. Bonner Johnson <www.assess.nelson.com/test-ind/wj-3-cog.html>	

Pearson Acronyms

<www.pearsonassessments.com/hai/SimpleProductListing.
aspx?Mode=acronym&Section=C>

Appendix A

Guess the Covered Word

The volcano is erupting.

1. Cover the word "erupting." Have students brainstorm a list of what word would make sense there.

2. Uncover the first letter of the word (i.e., the *e* in erupting)

3. Have the student revise their list. If student hasn't guessed the word, reveal the next letter, and so on.

The idea is to get students to combine thinking about context and phonic clues!

Appendix A.1

Portage & Main Press, 2013, *Resource Teachers*, ISBN: 978-1-55379-501-8

Click and Clunk Card

When I don't know a word I can...

1. Look at the picture for clues.

2. Slow down and reread the sentence, and think about what would make sense here.

3. Look for small words in a bigger word or break the word into parts.

4. Sound out the word.

5. Skip the word and read on to get more clues.

Appendix A.2

Portage & Main Press, 2013, *Resource Teachers*, ISBN: 978-1-55379-501-8

VAKT

Visual, Auditory, Kinesthetic, Tactile

1. Choose a word or words — no more than 3 to 5.

2. Teacher prints the word on the board, while saying the word and then the letters aloud.

   e.g., *"when, w-h-e-n, when"*

3. The student traces over the letters 5 times, while saying the word and the letters aloud.

   e.g., while tracing *"when, w-h-e-n, when,"* x 5

4. Teacher asks the student to take a picture of the word in their mind, then close their eyes. With eyes closed, the student says the word and spells it out aloud.

   "when, w-h-e-n, when"

5. While the student still has their eyes closed, the teacher erases the word from the board.

6. Then, teacher asks the student to open their eyes, print the word on the board, while saying first the word, then the letters aloud.

   "when, w-h-e-n, when"

If the student is not able to do so, repeat steps 1 through 5.

Appendix A.3

Appendix B

Student Survey:

Developmental Characteristics of Gifted Children

Please check all that apply

Intellectual Development:

_____ 1. I can explain my ideas easily – I know more words than other kids my age

_____ 2. I have an excellent memory

___✓___ 3. I learn things quickly, usually the first time someone shows me or tells me

___✓___ 4. I am very curious, and I get really into things when I am interested in them

___✓___ 5. I am a divergent thinker (one thing connects to another, and I see how they are alike when others don't)

___✓___ 6. I like to solve challenging, complex problems

___✓___ 7. I prefer to make my own choices, rather than having the teacher tell me how to do it

In Music ___ 8. I persevere (keep going) when things are challenging

___✓___ 9. I am a perfectionist, I get frustrated or down on myself when things don't turn out exactly how I wanted them to

___✓___ 10. I love to read, I read a lot!

Imaginational / Creative Development:

___✓___ 1. I use metaphors (I compare one thing to another) a lot when I talk / write

___✓___ 2. I have a great imagination, I invent things, like fantasy, magic, other worlds, etc.

___✓___ 3. I have unique problem solving strategies – I solve things in ways others don't

___✓___ 4. I can visualize things in great detail (see pictures / images in my head)

___✓___ 5. I perceive things in poetic / dramatic ways (I can see the feelings, imagine what it's like)

___✓___ 6. I remember my dreams in great detail

___✓___ 7. Sometimes I mix my fantasy worlds / ideas with reality

___✓___ 8. People say I am very creative

Appendix B.1

Portage & Main Press, 2013, *Resource Teachers*, ISBN: 978-1-55379-501-8

Emotional / Social Development:

_____ 1. My feelings go from high to low really strongly (ie I am very happy / excited, or very
sad / upset)

__✓__ 2. I feel things really deeply about my friends and family

__✓__ 3. I am really aware of myself – I know what I am thinking and feeling more than most

__✓__ 4. I am very empathic – I feel what others are feeling, am concerned for other people and
what's happening in the world

__✓__ 5. My feelings sometimes get expressed in my body (eg I get headaches, stomach aches
when I am upset)

_____ 6. I show my feelings to others – I don't hide them, or can't hide them

__✓__ 7. When I remember things that happened before, I can still remember how I felt

__✓__ 8. I prefer to have one or two close friends than lots of casual friends

__✓__ 9. I often relate better to adults or kids who are older than me

__✓__ 10. I often feel like I don't fit in, that I am different

__✓__ 11. It is important to me that things are fair and just

_____ 12. I think respect is earned, I don't just listen because adults say so

Psychomotor Development:

_____ 1. I can use my left or right hands

_____ 2. I talk fast

_____ 3. I have a lot of energy, get excited easily

_____ 4. I am very competitive, do a lot of sports

__✓__ 5. I don't sleep very much

Sensory Development:

__✓__ 1. I am sensitive to smells, bright colors, loud noises, etc.

__✓__ 2. Art, music, and nature affect me emotionally

__✓__ 3. I get "sensory overload" (feel stressed out) in crowds, noise, heat, etc.

__✓__ 4. I get bored easily – I need constant activity

__✓__ 5. I am sensitive to touch (eg clothing tags bug me)

Appendix B.1

Portage & Main Press, 2013, *Resource Teachers*, ISBN: 978-1-55379-501-8

Teacher Survey:
Developmental Characteristics of Gifted Children

Emotional / Social Development:

_____ 1. The student's feelings go from high to low intensively (ie they are very happy / excited, or very sad / upset)

___✓___ 2. The student feels things really deeply about friends and family

___✓___ 3. The student is very self-aware – they know what they are thinking and feeling

___✓___ 4. The student is very empathic – they feel what others are feeling, are concerned for other people and what's happening in the world

___✓___ 5. The student's feelings sometimes get expressed in their body (eg get headaches, stomach aches when upset)

_____ 6. The student shows their feelings to others – they don't hide them, or can't hide them

_____ 7. When the student remembers things that happened before, they can still remember how it felt

___✓___ 8. The student prefers to have one or two close friends than lots of casual friends

___✓___ 9. The student often relate better to adults or kids who are older than them

___✓___ 10. The student often feels like they don't fit in, that they are different

___✓___ 11. It is important to the student that things are fair and just

_____ 12. The student thinks respect is earned, they don't just listen because adults say so

Psychomotor Development:

_____ 1. The student can use their left or right hands

At times 2. The student talks fast

_____ 3. The student has a lot of energy, gets excited easily

_____ 4. The student is very competitive, does a lot of sports

__?___ 5. The student doesn't sleep very much

Sensory Development:

___✓___ 1. The student is sensitive to smells, bright colors, loud noises, etc.

___✓___ 2. Art, music, and nature affect the student emotionally

___✓___ 3. The student gets "sensory overload" (feel stressed out) in crowds, noise, heat, etc.

___✓___ 4. The student gets bored easily – he/she needs constant activity

_____ 5. The student is sensitive to touch (eg clothing tags bug them)

Appendix B.2

Portage & Main Press, 2013, *Resource Teachers*, ISBN: 978-1-55379-501-8

Please check all that apply

Intellectual Development:

_____ 1. The student can explain his/her ideas easily – He/she know more words than other kids their age

_____ 2. The student has an excellent memory

✓ 3. The student learns things quickly, usually the first time someone shows him/her

✓ 4. The student is very curious, and gets really into things when he/she is interested in them

✓ 5. The student is a divergent thinker (one thing connects to another, and they see how things are alike when others don't)

✓ 6. The student likes to solve challenging, complex problems

✓ 7. The student prefers to make their own choices

_____ 8. The student perseveres (keep going) when things are challenging

✓ 9. The student is a perfectionist, he/she get frustrated or down on him/her self when things don't turn out exactly how they wanted them to

✓ 10. The student loves to read

Imaginational / Creative Development:

✓ 1. The student uses metaphors (compares one thing to another) a lot when they talk / write

✓ 2. The student has a great imagination, they invent things, like fantasy, magic, other worlds, etc.

✓ 3. The student has unique problem solving strategies – they solve things in ways others don't

✓ 4. The student can visualize things in great detail (see pictures / images in their head)

✓ 5. The student perceives things in poetic / dramatic ways (they can see the feelings, imagine what it's like)

_____ 6. The student remembers their dreams in great detail

_____ 7. Sometimes the student mixes fantasy worlds / ideas with reality

✓ 8. The student is very creative in areas of interest / talent

Appendix B.2

Portage & Main Press, 2013, *Resource Teachers*, ISBN: 978-1-55379-501-8

Parent Survey:

Developmental Characteristics of Gifted Children

Emotional / Social Development:

_____ 1. My child's feelings go from high to low intensively (ie they are very happy / excited, or very sad / upset)

✓ 2. My child feels things really deeply about friends and family

✓ 3. My child is very self-aware – they know what they are thinking and feeling

✓ 4. My child is very empathic – they feel what others are feeling, are concerned for other people and what's happening in the world

✓ 5. My child's feelings sometimes get expressed in their body (eg get headaches, stomach aches when upset)

_____ 6. My child shows their feelings to others – they don't hide them, or can't hide them

✓ 7. When my child remembers things that happened before, they can still remember how it felt

✓ 8. My child prefers to have one or two close friends than lots of casual friends

✓ 9. My child often relate better to adults or kids who are older than them

✓ 10. My child often feels like they don't fit in, that they are different

✓ 11. It is important to my child that things are fair and just

_____ 12. My child thinks respect is earned, they don't just listen because adults say so

Psychomotor Development:

_____ 1. My child can use their left or right hands

_____ 2. My child talks fast

_____ 3. My child has a lot of energy, gets excited easily

_____ 4. My child is very competitive, does a lot of sports

✓ 5. My child doesn't sleep very much

Sensory Development:

✓ 1. My child is sensitive to smells, bright colors, loud noises, etc.

✓ 2. Art, music, and nature affect my child emotionally

✓ 3. My child gets "sensory overload" (feel stressed out) in crowds, noise, heat, etc.

✓ 4. My child gets bored easily – he/she needs constant activity

✓ 5. My child is sensitive to touch (eg clothing tags bug them)

Appendix B.3

Portage & Main Press, 2013, *Resource Teachers*, ISBN: 978-1-55379-501-8

Please check all that apply

Intellectual Development:

_____ 1. My child can explain his/her ideas easily – He/she know more words than other kids their age

__✓__ 2. My child has an excellent memory

__✓__ 3. My child learns things quickly, usually the first time someone shows him/her

__✓__ 4. My child is very curious, and gets really into things when he/she is interested in them

__✓__ 5. My child is a divergent thinker (one thing connects to another, and they see how things are alike when others don't)

__✓__ 6. My child likes to solve challenging, complex problems

__✓__ 7. My child prefers to make their own choices

_____ 8. My child perseveres (keep going) when things are challenging

__✓__ 9. My child is a perfectionist, he/she get frustrated or down on him/her self when things don't turn out exactly how they wanted them to

__✓__ 10. My child loves to read

Imaginational / Creative Development:

__✓__ 1. My child uses metaphors (compares one thing to another) a lot when they talk / write

__✓__ 2. My child has a great imagination, they invent things, like fantasy, magic, other worlds, etc.

__?__ 3. My child has unique problem solving strategies – they solve things in ways others don't

__✓__ 4. My child can visualize things in great detail (see pictures / images in their head)

__✓__ 5. My child perceives things in poetic / dramatic ways (they can see the feelings, imagine what it's like)

__✓__ 6. My child remembers their dreams in great detail

__✓__ 7. Sometimes my child mixes fantasy worlds / ideas with reality

__✓__ 8. People say my child is very creative

Appendix B.3

Portage & Main Press, 2013, *Resource Teachers*, ISBN: 978-1-55379-501-8